'WE THE RODENTS'

A Fairy Tale

By R. C. Seely

This book is dedicated to all those who, still have faith in our country. To those who think our best days are behind us, I hope this renews it.

R.C. Seely, the Author

CHAPTER ONE:

A NEW LIFE

It's been about seven years now since it happened, The

Year of the Rat, or to them, the Great Enlightenment of the Species.
A time of change in the very nature of their societal structure, their
understanding of the world around them. They are now experiencing
another election, the same as their counterpart species the Human
Race does.

At the first institution of this Era of change no one with any
knowledge of it would ever have believed that these two species could
cohabitate any longer. This is indeed a milestone in the history of
Rat-kind. To think it all started so innocently too. An awakening of
their potential that almost created a civil war between the species. At
one point an ever worse prospect for Human kind, at the policies of
the rodent's most feared dictator… The Human Genocide. With
their numbers they could have done it too. There was one rodent that
stood between this possibility, and a peaceful pact of intellectual being.
This is how it all began…

.. It was a calm night in the Manhattan Burroughs, and the clock ticking away is the only sound heard, in the apartment of Rachel and Connor Sims. In the other room lay their ten year old daughter Becky, sound asleep dreaming of fantastic adventures I'm sure, as that is what children do, and quite well at that.

Across the room in a wire cage lies her pet rat, who she affectionately named Jefferson, after the former president and diplomat. Being of a young age and not having any particular proclivity towards political issues, she did not name him that because of the man's accomplishments, but because she liked the name. Jefferson is the only creature in the dwelling that is not enjoying the comforts of sleep. He is wide awake, to the contrary, because an opportunity has come his way and he is pondering its implications. In her inattentive manner of many children, young Becky has failed to properly secure the latch on Jefferson's cage and he has just noticed this error.

Do I flee, leaving behind the comforts of this domestic life? The rodent considers to himself, *Or do I stay and enjoy an existence without fear of starvation or even more... predation? What a dilemma! Although I don't think that mighty urgent sense of curiosity will be satisfied with me staying in this cage... If I'm going to do this, I must do it now. Sorry, my dear,* he says to himself as though the child can hear his thoughts. *But this life is not for me. May you find another rodent who may be content, if not even happy, with this arrangement. I'm not meant to spend the rest of my life in a cage. Farewell.*

Without another moment's hesitation, Jefferson pushes on the

2

door. It opens with a crash, that was not anticipated and it was too loud for comfort. Jefferson freezes, as Becky looks up. Then she puts her head back down on the pillow and picks up where she left off in her dream. Jefferson sighs with relief and cautiously scampers out of his former prison.

Now what? he considers to himself. *Now I need to find a way out to the world. But where?* He sees his way out through a hole in the window screen. It's only about an inch, but that should be enough. Rats, like all rodents have a flexible skeleton and the skull is the only solid bone they have, so if that fits through, then the rest of their body should have no trouble whatsoever.

Focusing on the target Jefferson heads to the dresser, climbs up to the top of it, and leaps onto the window sill. He reaches the break in the screen and pushes it, enlarging the hole out to its maximum size. Without any problems to the plan, he climbs out and onto the ledge. Now to find a way to the ground. He surveys the area and assesses his options and there it is, on the next ledge, the fire escape. Just one more leap to freedom. One more leap to his new life. The thing is that's quite a leap, their apartment's on the fifth floor! If he doesn't stick the landing **all** his problems are over!

Well I didn't come this far to be stymied by a ledge. Here we go! With that he jumps and almost misses. Clinging for his life, Jefferson pulls himself unto the fire escape. From there he heads to his new life.

He spends the rest of that night exploring, taking in all the sights, sounds, and smells, that he has not been able to experience, despite being only a few feet away. *I'm no longer a domesticated rat,* he considers to himself, *I better start adapting to my new surroundings. After all, here only the strong and resourceful survive.*

So he starts adapting, first rummaging through trash cans in the city. He finds many goodies and gets them down. Then the next essential need.. Shelter. As he heads farther into the heart of the city, and farther from what was his home. He finds a hole in the wall of a large stone building. When he reaches it, he starts to smell inside before going in. *What is that aroma? I know it from somewhere, but I can't quite place it.* Left with the options of a convenient, yet unfamiliar dwelling, is still a better prospect than a night unprotected from the environment and the creatures on the prowl and it's starting to rain, is a consideration in favor of it as well. The final deciding factor however winds up being his natural rodent curiosity. So Jefferson squeezes through. As he goes farther down the hole the smell gets more and more abundant and oddly intoxicating.

At the end of the tunnel, the hole is partially blocked by part of the debris from the decay that formed the hole. With just a little bit effort the rat clears the path and enters. *That's it! I remember this smell now! I believe the humans call it, "paper."* Indeed we do, because that is what it is. Emanating from the wall to wall, books covering all the walls. Jefferson's ultimate scavenging endeavor has brought him to the public library. He looks inside and sees that the building is dark and no other creatures appear anywhere in sight. Hold it! He sniffs the air. Also no problem. Lastly, he holds perfectly still and waits for any stirrings. Nothing.

So before finding a burrow, for the rest of a long, but triumphant evening, he decides to explore. On the floor

4

someone has dropped a watch. He studies it for a moment, seeing if he can make sense out of the alien markings on its dial, or even its very purpose, for that matter. If he could have read it, he would have known that he had plenty of time to himself tonight. Since it was only eleven thirty-five. It would be hours before the first librarian would come.

He starts sniffing the air again, sees if there is anything to draw his interest. He scurries down the rows looking around. Then in the children's section, he finds a book that has fallen off the shelf. Still lugging the timepiece with him, the rat heads over to the book for further examination. He sniffs it and is just about to start gnawing at the binding, when the writing on the cover catches his eye. He has never actually paid any attention to what was on books before (his main interest was a biological need of keeping his teeth filed down to avoid any health maladies), but for some reason he finds himself mesmerized by it. Not unlike the encounter with the wristwatch when he first entered. He studies it, over and over again trying to crack the code, failing with each attempt.

In disgust he lets the book drop, with the force of the fall it splays open. Jefferson looks at it again. *More of these markings are inside? I never even thought of looking there.* On the open page was a single letter, a giant A. Jefferson's good fortune, it appears to have continued, the book is one made to help children learn the Alphabet. He focuses on the letter, storing it in memory. Then he follows it with his paw, retracing it over and again. Then he turns the page. He repeats this cycle with the next letter. He continues this through the night, until he hears something. The lock on the door is being turned, the door is being

5

opened. As quickly as he can he heads to the back to the hole he came in at, just barely avoiding being seen. He sets the watch down in the hole and heads out in the world to get some food.

After his foraging, Jefferson spends the rest of the day sleeping in the hole. He wakes up to the sound of the last librarian leaving. With the same caution he took the night before, he doesn't leave until sure it's safe. He steps out of the hole and goes exploring again. He leaps up unto the chair behind the counter, from there he climbs to the checkout counter to find more reading material.

He finds a book left on the counter and opens it up. It's a book about his namesake, Thomas Jefferson. Next to it are other books. The inquisitive rodent reads book after book until the first librarian starts her shift. He continues this for a couple of weeks; unmolested in his academic endeavors by his human hosts.

Then one day he notices an odd contraption on the floor. It has a wooden base with a wire and a spring at the back of it. On a small metal bracket is a piece of bread. Not being particularly foolish as rats go, he heads back to the den, which by this time he had made bigger in the dwelling itself though not altering the openings on either side to avoid detection. When he comes back he has the watch and pushes the leather band against the metal bracket. Suddenly the trap snaps on the wrist strap. Jefferson gets the strap out of the trap, grabs the bread, and goes about his normal routine. This goes on for a couple of months. The rat besting the trap, night after night. Then one day Jefferson has a very rude encounter, yes, very rude indeed.

CHAPTER TWO:

ENLIGHTENMENT

Jefferson was just starting his normal evening vigil,

when behind him he hears a loud thump (loud to him at any rate, though barely perceptible to humans), when he turns around to find a wall of fur. He looks up finding himself looking at a almost all white cat with the exception of a few markings, and an especially noticeable one, above the right eye.

The feline starts toward Jefferson and extends a paw to the rat. "Hello there. My name is Gorby, that's short for Gorbachev, I was named because of this odd marking on my head. It reminded my owner of the Russian leader, Mikhail Gorbachev. Anyway, what is your handle?" Gorby asks, in a booming voice (or booming to a rat anyway).

"My name is Jefferson, named after the second president

of the United States, Thomas Jefferson. My former owner just liked the name," Jefferson replied.

"Former owner. The lack of fear of people, that sense of curiosity over commonsense, I thought you might have been a 'Domestie.' Yes, now that I see you, it's very obvious. Wild rats don't have your markings," Gorby replied.

"Beg your pardon, for my ignorance. But what exactly is a 'Domestie'?" Jefferson asks.

"Oh my I'm sorry, how rude of me throwing out such terms. A 'Domestie' is the common street vernacular for a domesticated or formerly domesticated animal."

"I see, well I would like to stay and continue our conversation, titillating as it is. But if you excuse me I have a previous engagement, so could I get my paw back, and be on my way," Jefferson, calmly states.

"Oh I'm terribly sorry my little friend, but you will have to postpone your plans, for again sorry, indefinitely," Gorby, replies trying to sound polite.

"What do you mean?"

"I was brought in to eliminate the sudden rodent problem, sir. I intend to do it too," Gorby responds, this time far less cordially.

"So our pleasantries are at a conclusion I gather?" Jefferson asks.

"I'm afraid so."

"Well than I hope you understand what I'm about to do Gorby, as looking out for my own best interests."

"What-" before Gorby can finish his thought, Jefferson

chomps down on the cat's paw. "MEROWW!" the cat exclaims, howling in pain at the blow. Before Gorby can recover, Jefferson makes a dash for the other side of the building. "Vermin, you will regret that!" fumes the cat.

With his night after night of regular study Jefferson had learned a lot including the definition of many words, Vermin being among them. Understanding it's meaning now, he finds himself hurt by such an exclamation. The situation does not give him much time to reflect on that though, so he puts this aside for his more pressing need of self preservation.

For at that moment he has found a dark section behind some of the books on the lowest shelf of the bookcase, but that security won't last. Not with so active a predator in the building.

The only question is how long does he have to think before the chase begins again. The cat goes by the row where he's hiding and in a moment of panic, Jefferson reacts. He sudden barks as deeply as he can. Which must have been deep enough to be convincing, because when he scurries away, he looks back and sees Gorby has perched at the top of one of the bookcases, still in a state of alarm. This has bought him the time he needs and he sprints at full speed to his den. He dares not rest though, because the den doesn't offer much protection in the current situation. He grabs the watch and makes his exit.

Now homeless, Jefferson raids the first trashcan he sees before searching for a new den. He might be destitute, but at least he will be so with a full stomach. A banana peel and part of a gourmet hotdog. A feast for a king, if that king were a rat.

So with one need fulfilled, he continues his search for a

new dwelling.

Avoiding being seen for fear of predators and passing cars, the rodent goes down block after block in mad dashes. Greeted time after time with either a large beast trying to devour him or another of his own not in the mood to relinquish his section of real estate. In his quest, he finds himself in Riverside Park. He takes in a large breath, indulging in a new and very unfamiliar smell. This is the first time being surrounded by nature, you see. While it is unmistakable a virgin experience for him, it also feels strangely like coming home. Searching near the trees, he finds one with the roots penetrating the soil and a hole already formed. It doesn't go very deep, but it will serve very well. Very well, indeed. Jefferson slips into it and curls up as tightly as possible to conserve heat, and falls asleep.

The next morning Jefferson is awakened by the call of a pigeon, above him in the tree. They must have a nest in in one of the branches. He gives himself a well earned stretch before exploring. He is in need of sustenance after the disastrous encounter last night, as he used up a lot of energy. So he heads to the nearest trashcan to forage. While in his search for food, he comes across something else that perks his interest.

"W-Wall Str-reet J-J-Jour-nal," he reads aloud. "Wall Street Journal. Bless my good luck! It's a newspaper," he shouts with joy, leaping into the air with excitement. He grabs a few scraps of food, and the paper, and rushes back to the hole in the tree. Still trembling with excitement, he doesn't know which to consume first, the food or the paper. "Easy boy, the newsprint can wait. The food must be taken care of before

10

others sense its aroma."

With that Jefferson starts eating, not realizing until now that he is actually quite famished. After finishing his breakfast, he starts looking through the newspaper. Page after page, article after article, every word, every ad. He then rereads the parts that he couldn't completely follow, until it makes sense, or as much as it can make sense of at least. When he finishes with the newsprint, he uses it to line the walls of his den. He places the watch towards the back of his den and reads the time from it. Nine thirty. He puts it away and goes to the entrance of the hole. He rests on the roots that guard his new home and just watches the world around him. "I wonder where my path is to take me next?" he asks, to nobody in particular. But that's a question to be answered another day.

For the next couple of weeks Jefferson is allowed some respite from the chaos that most other rats must endure and once again has a certain amount of routine to his life. He goes from one trashcan to another, for food and reading material, usually nothing too exceptional of either. A bag of left-over candy bar, and a New York Times. Some frozen yogurt, and a Crosswords book. One day he did luck out and found some popcorn shrimp and a pocket book of the U.S. Constitution. That was a day that changed his life again. He studied that little booklet over and over, until he had it memorized better than most human lawmakers or politicians. It started sparking a real change in him. He started seeing the way Rat-kind lives in a whole new way and it left him wondering if there could be more to life. *Could we have what the humans have? A civilization,*

11

a sophisticated culture. We have the advantage that we could
use the portions of their model that works and abandon the
parts that don't.

For the moment that was an inquiry that would have to be academic, seeing as it was just him at the moment and a society is by definition not a single entity. He spends the rest of the afternoon in reflection of this, while vacantly watching the other wildlife in their daily struggle for survival. It occurs to him, the human world isn't as far from the animal one as they like to think. The strongest and most prosperous social structures are the ones that encourage self reliance and in order to do that you must embrace individualism and defend your own self interest. The first law of nature- Only the strong will survive. The next day Jefferson decides to start his path on this road of what he calls, 'The Great Rodent Enlightenment' , and starts drafting a set of governing principles. 'The Rodent Life Documents', he calls them.

All Rodents possess a certain innate understanding of things, matched only by the Human species and with this understanding comes certain ethical judgments, based on core principles, that need to be made. These ethical considerations need to be in line with the following principles to maintain our emerging society and for prosperity to occur.

1st No rodent shall kill another. We are no
      longer bound strictly to the laws of nature,
      but one of ethical thought, word, and deed.
      We must act in accordance to this.

2nd Rodents are not to take advantage of each
      other. We are to help each other and
      community action is encouraged.

3rd An impartial court is to be established, in
      our Rodent Society, to protect the rights of
      the individual Rodent, in cases in which a
      fair compromise cannot be reached.

4th No Rodent shall kill any other Natural
      Being, including any and all Human Beings.
      Some Rodents have been mistreated by them
      but this does not excuse retaliation against
      them and such crimes will be strictly
      punished.

5th Entrepreneurship and Industry shall be
      rewarded in our society. The goal of our
      Rodent Society is to become self sufficient
      and not rely on the Humans at some point.

Then and only then will we be a truly free
society.

6th All Rodents have the right to defend themselves against other Rodents, Humans, or
their own Government. All Rodents also
maintain privacy from government as well.

7th All Rodents are encouraged to learn to read
and write. As well as other educational
endeavors.

8th All Rodents are encouraged to participate in
the election of their representatives and run
for political positions as well.

These are the Rights and Responsibilities in
our Rodent Society, to be defended tooth and claw,
by the Representatives and at times the Society itself.
This is the beginning of a new era. The beginning of
the Rodent Society. So we come together in the desire
of prosperity, we come together united yet individuals,
we come together as friends and brethren. We come
together because, We the Rodents, say we must.

Jefferson Rat

14

After its completion Jefferson is beaming, thinking

of the implications of this document. Its significance for good. Its simplicity. Now he understands his namesake and wants to do him proud.

His daydreaming does have its limits however and it soon is interrupted by a disturbance a few feet away. A bunch of squirrels are chasing a rat on the green grass of the mid-afternoon. Feeling a sudden sense of solidarity towards this stranger Jefferson joins in the action, to assist the outnumbered rodent. He follows behind the pack, looking around for an opportunity to turn the tides in the rat's favor.

Think, Jefferson, Think...

He keeps up his pace with the pack and in a moment of insanity, leaps up and lands on the back of the closest squirrel.

To make sure the squirrel goes where he wants, he grabs the squirrel's whiskers, using them like reins. He then coerces his ride to speed ahead of his cohorts and makes a sharp turn, sending the other squirrels flying in all directions. Still on his mount, he grabs the rat that was the pursuit of the pack.

"You okay?" Jefferson asks.

"Yes," the other rat replies.

"What's your name?" Jefferson asks.

"My what?" he answers.

"Your name. Mine's Jefferson. Don't you have one?"

"No, we 'Wilds' don't have names. Are you a

'Domestie'?"

"Yes, I used to be a human's pet, but I left a couple of months ago."

"What's a month?" the other rat asks.

"It's a way to measure time."

"Oh. I see."

Jefferson then sees the opportunity he had been looking for, with an open soup can a few feet ahead.

"Hold on tight. This could be bad."

Jefferson wraps his tail around the squirrel's front leg and as planned the squirrel goes into a skid, and his crashes into the can headfirst.

"Let's go. His buddies will be here any minute."

The two rats hide behind a bush narrowly missing being seen by the squirrels; fortunately, their attention is focused on their comrade with his head stuck in the soup can. Jefferson and the unnamed rodent take their leave and head back to Jefferson's den.

"So why were they chasing you?" Jefferson asks.

"Because this is their territory. This park is their foraging ground. How about you, Jefferson, what's your story?"

"I told you, I left my cage and I've been living wild for a couple of months."

"You haven't told me everything. You're obviously not using this newspaper as den lining. This has been cherished."

Jefferson puts his paw to his face in contemplation. "Okay.. You're right I haven't been entirely upfront with you," Jefferson starts, "Before I tell you, let me ask you a question."

16

"Okay, ask away," the other rat says.

"Have you ever wondered if there could be anything more?"

"What do you mean?" the unnamed stranger asks, obviously perplexed by the inquiry with an expression on his face to match.

"I mean the daily struggle, eat, sleep, reproduce, find shelter, avoid predators. Is that it, or could we have something more?"

"I don't know I guess, I've never thought about it."

"Well, neither did I until now…"

For his new acquaintance, Jefferson goes through the events of the past couple of months. From his escape, to his time at the library, to his encounter with Gorbie, to the 'Rodent Enlightenment' and the birth of the 'Rodent Life Document.'

"So you just had a cognitive awakening?" asks the stranger after the recollection.

"Basically yes. Look, how surprising is that, really in the grand scheme of things? The only thing that separates the Humans from the rest of the Animal Kingdom, is mental aware -ness and a moral code… How is this any different?"

"Because we are rats."

"Rats are smart, calculating, articulate beings. Sound familiar?"

17

"Okay… Good point. So what are you saying exactly?" the stranger asks.

"I'm saying we could have what they have. We could create our own culture, our own advanced society. Our own enterprises and industry. Our own works of art. Our own works of literature. Our own courts and laws. You name it, we make it."

"You know how this sounds, right? I need more to convince me." Jefferson goes to the back of the den and grabs a piece of paper, he opens it up and shows it to the unnamed rat.

"You can read it?" he asks Jefferson.

"I wrote it."

"This is the 'Rodent Life Document'? So it is real."

"Yes, and I can teach you to read it."

So he begins his tutelage of the unnamed stranger

and explains the importance of individualizing, and they start to find him a name. After a lot of reflection, the settled handle is 'Madison', after James Madison.

For the next week that is how things went for the two rodents studying the practical aspects of the their future society.

Figuring out ways to turn these grandiose visions into a possibility.

T hen the day came when Madison had left when

foraging and was gone for many days. Jefferson was concerned not only because he hoped nothing had happened to his new found colleague and friend, but also because he did not want to suffer through loneliness now that he had so much to offer. So he did what anyone, rat, human, or whatever other natural being would do, he went foraging. He would look for food, and a scrap of some sort of reading material to occupy his busy mind.

This continued without any one to keep himself company, but he never faltered at his duty to himself, or his future civilization, writing more rodent laws and drafting the 'Rodent Right's.'

After a week's passing as suddenly as he had disappeared, Madison returned. "Hello, my friend," he called out joyously.

"Hello Madison. Where have you been?"

"Jefferson, you're not angry with me are you? I didn't mean to upset you, dear boy."

"No, I was merely bothered with how abruptly you had vanished. I thought maybe another squirrel had gotten you. You know for a 'Wild' you're not very good at defending yourself."

"Now, now, there's no need to insult me. Besides I have a surprise for you."

19

Now Jefferson's trying to be nonchalant about this, sticking with his bravado of anger. Unfortunately, as with many mammals with tails, his gives him away, displaying his curiosity.

"How would you like to test your Rodent Society model?"

"What do you mean, Madison?" Jefferson asks, abandoning what is left of his flimsy facade.

"I found our new home," Madison replies smiling.

It seems that while he was foraging, Madison had

lost his way, while being chased by a Rottweiler. He searched and searched for the park, stopping only for food and rest.

Two days had passed and still no park, then on the third day he came upon what he believed to be home, but it was another park. He knew for sure because of the lack of squirrels and the new scents in the air. In his journey of exploration, he did find inhabitants; a group of rats. They took him to their lair that lay underneath the park and treated him like one of their own kin. He spent the next couple of days talking to them about Jefferson's venture with great interest.

"**So, they're really onboard** with it?" Jefferson asks

while they make their way to their new home.

"Oh yes. It seems their last patriarch has passed on and they are looking to restructure their society."

"It's a good thing that it was us that came across them then. A less civilized rat might have taken advantage of them," Jefferson says more to himself than to Madison.

"What do you mean?" Madison asks.

"Oh..." Jefferson responds clearly not expecting a comment from his travel companion. " Nothing.. I was just thinking about the history of the humans and how many times their culture could have advanced if not for domineering leaders. Adolf Hitler, Josef Stalin, Mao, Napoleon Bonaparte, the Roman Emperors, all had two things in common. They took advantage of their people and they coveted power. Some of them might have had the best of intentions in the beginning, but it all ended up the same.

The dictators are gone and the country's in ruin. It's tragic and such a waste. They cared more about the power than the people and that could easily have transferred to any species. It's basically a simple tribal structure society, wrapped up in a false package of civility and justice. It's really just the opposite though."

"Yeah, that was my thought too," Madison replies dryly.

Jefferson just gives him a quizzical look and chuckles.

21

As night approaches, the two rats bunk down in a hole in the wall of a building along the way. Using an old discarded sock, that Jefferson brought as a kind of makeshift backpack for his writings and watch, the rodents have a pillow. They awaken from the sun greeting them from their temporary den and grab some food, with stomachs, full they set off. Now if they didn't live in a place like New York, with it's jaded attitudes and a utter lack of curiosity; some would wonder about a rodent with a backpack, and if so they might hinder their advancement in this trip. But thankfully they do, and the two travelers journeyed on unmolested.

After about half a days traveling they reach their destination and instinctively head for the nearest bush. Jefferson set down his bag and rests for a few a minutes. Not being in much better shape, Madison follows suit.

A few minutes later Jefferson is awakened by a rustling of the bush, he turns to find Madison has gone. *Great, I don't know my way around, and I don't know what's moving out there, and I'm facing it alone. What else?* That's when Madison suddenly leaps out and lands on top of a very surprised Jefferson. "Awake yet," Madison asks.

"Yes, I do believe I am.. Could you get off me now?"

"Right… Sorry. Are you ready?"

"Ready for what?" Jefferson asks, brushing the dust from his fur.

"To meet our constituency."

"They're here?" Jefferson asks.

"They're here," Madison replies.

CHAPTER THREE:

THE SOCIETY

The first year of the colony was one of amazing

growth and the start of something better for every member there. Among those in the magistrate was of course Jefferson and Madison, but about fifty others also. Seeing as 'Wilds' typically didn't have names to start off, Jefferson helped them read and write and choose their identities.

Some picked older identities of the ancient philosophers like Plato or Aristotle. Some picked from the Roman Emperors such as Caesar, Nero, or Maximus.

Some took suit from Jefferson and Madison, they decided on the names of representatives like Hancock, Adams, Monroe, and Washington. Others picked from the list of more recent legislators like Clinton, Kerry, and Kennedy.

The other non political rodents decided their identities as well, with more common names, such as Smith, Connors, Tyler, or Michael.

One particularly mean rat, an old, wrinkled, basically hair-less creature, chose the name Soros. Another decided on

Trump, for some unknown reason they didn't really trust each other.

For any rodents I did fail to mention it was not meant to diminish their contribution to the colony or to the story they were just not mentioned. No disrespect was intended.

After that the rodents held their first elections for their representatives, senators and the 'Rodent Leader'. Courts have also been implemented and judges placed. The basis for their economy has started as well with the efforts of a few of the more industrious and managerial members of the Manhattan Colony, as they agree to be referred. For now the currency is the trade of food, for goods and services.

Some of the rodents have taken the step of manufacturing clothing, using dryer lint and superglue. The higher end suits go for a melon rind, or a couple of grapes. Basic clothing for corn kernels, potato chips, or a piece of hot dog. Whatever the seller is willing to barter down to though is the standard really, and some are by far more generous.

The 'Industrial' rodents have taken to the employing others in the occupation of dwelling construction, for those in the Manhattan Colony that are better off than others. Those not of the upper food thresh hold, barter on the price of property and sell it to them, by the 'Industrials,' to fix up.

Six months have now passed and the colony is

showing signs of prosperity. It's not total harmony however

and some of the rats are causing discord in the communities. There was a storm of political unrest with the results of the 'Rodent Leader' election outcome. It was rumored that Kerry was going to win and a rift ensued when Adams was declared the victor. Leading the charge of fraud was Nero, Caesar, and Soros.

In the wake of which, the division brought about a new concept, of 'Groups'. The first is the 'Originals' or the founders and policy makers of the original social structure designed by Jefferson and the 'Hoarders', a new Group dedicated to the act of self preservation and keeping the colony structure closer to its more wild roots rather than advancement towards an industrial civilization.

Then it happened. The single act that would change everything forever. Some rogue squirrels from the upper portion of the park destroyed part of the Manhattan Colony structure by knocking a tree branch onto a weaker part of the cavern. Angered by this, Adams declares war on the squirrels without even a discussion with the other representatives.

In a baffling act the Rodent Leader doesn't declare war on the squirrels at the upper end of the park but at the LOWER end of the park. The reason stated being that the squirrels at the lower end were the real perpetrators and the upper enders were the fall guys, despite the lack of evidence to support such claims. Fearing all his efforts of the past few months being threaten by Adams, Jefferson confronts him.

"What is going on here Adams? The Lower enders being the perpetrators and the Upper ender taking the wrap? Where's

25

the evidence? Please explain this lunacy to me."

"I don't believe I have to explain myself to you Jefferson. This is my administration, and if I feel this is the only way to protect the colony's inhabitants is to neutralize the squirrel invasion, that is what I will do."

"First off, being a member of this colony I AM entitled to an explanation. But more than that, you completely circumvented the Senators and our policy makers. Our laws don't grant you carte blanc when it comes to these matters. Also being one of your strongest supporters, colleague, and friend, I think I am entitled to know your logic of this decision."

Adams pauses and considers this for a moment, before turning from Jefferson. Adams lets out a sigh and responds.

"You're right, you do deserve more than just diatribe after all you've done… The upper end of the park has been stripped of resources, even the squirrels are having a hard go there.. I needed a validation for going into the lower end for food and other essentials, this attack was just that."

"You're telling me you're trying to justify the loss of rodent life, to validate the policies of callously plundering the innocent of their hard earned inventory? Is that what you're saying?"

"I'm saying that I'm securing the Manhattan Colony's survival," Adams snaps coldly.

Jefferson closes his eyes, trying to calm himself while he mentally digests what he has just heard.

Then he responses to Adams, "Well then I have to ask… If you take that position with your actions, where does this

violation of 'Rodent's Rights' end? Will you treat the rights of
 our citizens with such indifference? When one of the laws on
the books to protect them, gets in your way will you ignore it as
well?.."

  "Of course not Jefferson. I do this for them, after all."

  "You swore an oath to protect the rights of ALL rodents,
 not just the ones you deem worthy of your compassion."

  "I also promised to protect the colony against all threats
foreign and domestic. That, how I see it, is what I'm doing.
Good day, Mr. Statesrat."

  "Good day too you as well, Mr. Rodent Leader."

Still **fuming and muttering** (only the random expletives

being decipherable as language) to himself as he was leaving the
Rodent Leader lair, Jefferson doesn't notice Madison walk up
beside him.

  "Hello, Jefferson. How are you today?"

  "Hello, Madison. I'm alright, just trying to understand
how so clever a rat can come to such a moronic conclusion."

  "Adams, you mean?"

  "Who else? Invading a guiltless pack of squirrels for their
reserves, while letting the guilty roam untouched.. Is that really
 who our friend is?.."

  "So he confirmed it. I thought that was just lies by Soros
and Nero. I never would have believed it either."

  Jefferson stops, at this revelation, "Soros and Nero, what
are you talking about?"

27

"They have been telling all the other members of the colony that Adams's got to go, it was right before they left."

"They left?.. Where did they go? When did they leave?"

"A couple of days ago, they said something about finding Adams' replacement after his term."

"That can't be good Madison."

"What do you mean, Jefferson? You just said you weren't happy about Adams's conduct during this debacle."

"Adams didn't handle this situation well. He's not perfect, but who is. He at least has been trying to improve the lives of the citizens of the Manhattan Colony, whomever Soros backs will not take that kind of attitude. Look at his last endorsement, that potential dictator Kerry. No, this is not good at all."

"Well he still has the next year and half to turn things around."

It was decided that since a rodent's lifetime usually peaks around twelve, a two year term as Rodent Leader would be long enough, instead of the human US President's four year term. Just as with human's though, the 'Rodent Leader' can get in for a second term. However it should be noted that even in just two years time, a lot of damage can be caused by a very zealous rat.

Jefferson and Madison, in the predicament of having a bad, but well intentioned and familiar rat, or a possibly worse, not well intentioned and questionable rodent, decides that sticking behind Adams is the safer course of action. So they defend him. All the while hoping they can guide him back to the pathway of prosperity, that has always been their intentions. That is not the course that Adams has in mind though.

Instead of abandoning his agenda to go after the resources of the squirrels and try to figure a compromise with them, he strengthens his resolve and goes even harder at them, sending in a rat army to disarm them. In the end a rodent civil war ensues, pitting squirrel against rat, and threatening all the animals of the park. Many of the other residents make the conclusion that it is in their best interests to pick a side and most join the squirrels. Now the squirrels have most of the insects and the birds on their side as well. Pigeons dive bomb dropping their waste on the rat army, and the swarms of flies and hornets mercilessly tear through the troops.

On the other side the rats have the mice and sparrows, both tired of the bullying they have had to endure from the squirrels. With the advantage on the side of the squirrels, many a rat has lost his life for this cause.

This still doesn't lessen Adams' resolve and he sends in more troops, and trades more food for war supplies. The ingenuity of the more industrious rodents goes into the weapons business, creating new innovations of destruction. Sticks and rocks are of course the most basic and earlier implements, but there are now blades being fashioned in the hopes of decimating the squirrels and ending in rat victory for the Manhattan Colony.

"No longer are the rodent's united," Jefferson laments.

29

"I thought we wanted the residents of the Colony to think for themselves. Are they not doing that?" Madison asks.

"They are not THINKING period, that's the problem. When I started this society, I wanted it to take the best traits of the human culture to adopt, not the worst. Rather than talking to the squirrels, finding a solution that benefits both sides, we have gone straight for the throat. Deliver the kill shot as it were. Adams has twisted everything I have tried to build and turned it into a weapon against our fellow rodent."

"So what do we do?"

"I wish I knew Madison... We need to try to reason with him again. Through his mate this time.. Abigail might get through to him, I don't think this is what she envisioned either."

"It's definitely worth a shot!" Madison pipes in.

"It might be our last shot, is what I'm afraid of.."
The two rats walk into the home of the Rodent Leader, to find him not at home, but thankfully his mate is.

"Hello, Madison, Jefferson, my mate is not at home, but my assistant tells me that he was not the one you wanted to see. So what could I do for you two such fine gentle-rats?"

"Abigail, we have known you and Adams for quite some time now. We know you both to be rats of high character and only want the best for the Colony, that is why we implore you to talk to your mate about ending this war. We fear that it can do the Colony nothing but harm and whatever benefits come from it do not outweigh the costs. Please.. Please, help him see reason.."

30

"I don't know that I can, but I will try. My dear sirs, because I do feel that you are more knowledgeable in these matters. I will talk to him, I promise."

"Thank you, Abigail," Jefferson says, while bowing.

"Yes, Thank You," Says Madison, doing the same.

For awhile the two rats walk in silence, after leaving the Rodent Leader's home, until Madison finally asks the question burning his brain.

"Jefferson, what do think will happen now?"

"I think Adams will do what he's doing now.."

"Then why did we even bother!" Madison replies, obviously angered.

"Because we have to do what we can, Madison. Adams does still have his civil side and she could bring it out."

"So we wait?" Madison asks.

"So we wait.."

Silence returns as the two walk down another trail, in the under -ground city.

"Want to get a drink?" Madison asks.

"Never wanted one more, my friend," Jefferson says, grabbing Madison's shoulder. "But not too much, we have a journey ahead of us tomorrow."

"Oh? Where pray tell are we going?"

"To the library."

The next day Jefferson and Madison start their

31

journey to the library, Madison is nowhere near as eager as his friend and mentor.

"Why exactly are we going to this domicile of death? If you don't mind telling me I would really like to know, before I sacrifice myself to this.. This.. Cat-demon, this Gorby."

This assessment makes Jefferson chuckle.

"Being a little melodramatic, aren't we. Besides, our future depends on knowledge of the past, this home of books is where will we find it."

"I'm not being melodramatic… I'm being realistic, and I just don't think this feline will be all that cooperative is all I'm saying. He did try to kill you once remember."

"That's a complication, I'll admit, but we will figure something out. We always do Madison, where's your faith in our cause?"

"I have faith we will be in a cat's digestive tract, that's what I have faith in."

"Who knows?.. Maybe he'll be more amiable, since he's had a chance to cool down."

Madison just gives Jefferson a skeptical look in response.

"What? Stranger things have happened, I've read about them… Did you ever read about this thing called the 'Fiji Mermaid.'"

"No and I don't think that I want to hear about it right now."

Jefferson ignores Madison's comment and continues.

"It was this exhibit, that the Barnum Circus had on

display… At first no one knew what it was and the audiences thought it was a legitimate mermaid, it was later revealed to be a hoax. That someone took a dead monkey that was dried up and had a fish sewn to it's back end and sold it to the circus. Isn't that bizarre!"

"Fascinating," Madison replies indifferently.

Madison and Jefferson spend the night in an alley along the way, first finding some food before finding a shelter for the night. The two rodents wake when the sun comes up, find some food, and start up their quest again. At first they are in quiet contemplation but as the day drags on they pick up debates on different topics. As the sun falls they find another temporary home and food.

The next day they start early again and it's not long before the library comes into view. As they get closer to the building, the rodent's hearts start racing faster and faster. Jefferson starts looking around the building for the hole in the wall and quickly finds it.

"Are you ready, Madison?"

"No. But let's do it anyway."

"That's the spirit."

Jefferson sneaks into the building first, pokes his head into the library and sniffs the air. When he's sure the coast is clear he signals Madison.

They enter the building and start exploring, keeping eyes

and ears at full alert for the cat.

"So where is he?"

"I don't know. Maybe the librarians got rid of him when I left.."

"You're not that lucky!" says a booming voice behind them.

It's Gorby and he's now blocking their exit. Madison is about to flee, when Jefferson grabs his tail.

"Are you MAD? Let's go!!" Madison exclaims passionately.

"No.. We must try to negotiate with him first."

"I don't know how to negotiate with teeth."

"Claim down, Madison. We'll see what happens."

"Do you wish to speak to me? Gorby asks. "Make it quick and I hope it's significant, seeing as it will be your last words."

"Yes. I do have something to discuss with you. First of all I hope you're not holding a grudge about what happened a few months ago. I was just doing what was necessary for my own survival."

"Hold a grudge… No, not at all," says the cat, lifting a paw at the same time. It was the paw with the bite marks, that had apparently left a scar. The cat then releases his claws and all but one of the mangled digit appears. The bite must have caused nerve damage to the paw.

"Oh, I see… Well, then I'll get right to the point. We are in a little bit of a conundrum and we need access to the books of this fine establishment. I understand your, shall we

34

say, reluctance, to be of service, however, I do believe we can reach an accord."

"I don't, but go on," says Gorby, impatiently.

"Really? I thought you could've seen it on your own… Well, then never mind. Let's just proceed with the chase then."

"See what? What am I not seeing?" responds Gorby angrily, baring his teeth.

"Well, as I was commenting to my friend, Madison, when we came in. I was not sure that the owners had kept you on after my departure. It is good to see they did, by the way. It was just a thought that occurred to me, that if you didn't have anymore rodents to vacate, it might be you who they let go. Oh, but I was being silly. So let's just continue with the chase, Gorby, and forget I said anything…"

Gorby is already considering what Jefferson has been saying though, and is not wanting to chase at the moment.

"Okay, I have thought about what you have been saying. I don't understand where you come into the equation. How can you help me avoid being tossed out into the street?" A smile crosses Jefferson lips. "Well," he continues. "The only way you can change that possible fate, is if you still have rodents to evict from the premises."

"Yes, my job is to get rid of vermin, but if there's vermin in the building how does that protect me?"

"Gorby, I'm trying to help. There's no need for using such derogatory slurs. Let's keep things civil… Yes, your job is to get rid of the RODENTS," Jefferson says placing emphasis

35

on the word rodent. "If the librarians see evidence of an epidemic, than yes, they will throw you out. However, if they find a TOTAL lack, of rodents, they might also assess you are no longer needed. The trick here is to find that happy medium between the two. So here's my proposal. We could come at night to do our research and periodically we will have a volunteer rat serve as a pest to be evicted by you during the day and afternoons. Just go to a dark corner of the building and release him."

"I'm afraid I can't go along with this plan, rodent."

"Why not?" Jefferson asks puzzled by the response.

"I will be evicted if I allow you access to these books. I know what your kind do to them, the collection will be destroyed in a month."

"Gorby, I promise, on my own life that no harm shall come to these books. We need them for research purposes only."

"Why?" Gorby asks.

"Can you read and write, Gorby?"

"Most certainly not."

"Want to learn?"

Gorby proved to be as fast a learner as Madison

or any of the other rodents for that matter. Madison and Jefferson did their studies at night and every once and a while would let Gorby 'catch' them for his owners benefit. While they studied they would help Gorby learn to read and write as well. They continued this for a couple of months until they made a decision and a heartbreaking one at that. They had to go back and they had no answer.

"We must go back and save our Colony, Gorby, but we will come back. In the mean time we will send other Statesrats, in our place. Maybe they can come up with something. For now farewell."

"Good bye, Jefferson and Madison. I will see you soon."

It was a quiet journey back, with a feeling of failure coming from the two rats. They stopped only for food and rest, and the rest was very uneasy. The only time anything was said was when they came back to the Colony.

"It's good to be back."

"Indeed."

"Do you have any ideas, Madison?"

"No... Do you?"

"Just, one.. Let the rodents decide the fate of the Colony. That's all we can do really. It's the rodent's house, after all." Madison just lets out a sigh of resignation at that comment.

What will be the Colony's fate, is the thought rushing through their minds.

CHAPTER FOUR:

A NEWCOMER

For the most part, the rest of the Adams's first term

wasn't different from the way it began. More wars against the

squirrels, regulating the industries have become the norm for

industry in the Colony.

The 'Hoarders' group has grown larger and more

organized with the unrest caused by Adams. The success of

the new society has gotten a large following of the rodents

migrating to the Colony. Many of the mice and squirrels have

joined, because of rights that its leaders have promised. But

more are given to these newcomers that are not extended to the

residents, this stand creates contention in the 'Hoarders' and

there is a split in both groups, creating other groups. None have

the numbers or power of the 'Hoarders' or 'Originals,' though.

These new groups are not without power or influence however, and should not be underestimated.

All the problems caused by Adams aside, the Colony isn't suffering all that much though. Prosperity and a certain amount of camaraderie is around. Many of the inhabitants have enjoyed a sense of accomplishment and are seeing the fruits of their labor.

As is the case in most instances though, you let down your guard, that's when a crisis occurs. A part of the structure at the back end of the Colony wasn't secured properly and it collapses. The emergency system in place is called into action, but mistakes are made. Many of the resident Rodents loss their homes and many have lost their lives. The destruction of property is catastrophic, but is nothing compared to the accusations of incompetence and blame catapulted at Adams and the 'Originals.' The 'Hoarders' have taken the action that Jefferson was most afraid of.. played politics.

"I knew this was going to happen, I just was hoping that we could have avoided it for awhile. Curse that sniffling coward, Kerry and his supporters. They just can't let it go, he lost. Get over it," Jefferson says, in his tirade to Madison.

"It had to happen, that is the nature of the beast."

"I know. I know. I'm just astounded by their level of animosity towards Adams, yes he could have gotten in faster. But he did something. None of them with their resources and 'good intentions' even tried."

"They see it as the 'Rodent-ment's' responsibility and

39

they did not feel it proper to get involved."

"I know, that's the excuse they use at least. I think they just want to see failure, so they can sweep in and take control."

"Jefferson, that's a horrible thing to say. We might disagree with them but they are still our brethren."

"We can't be afraid to consider the worst of them, if we don't all could be lost."

So the crisis continues and the grumbling from the 'Hoarders' does as well. Out of duty to their friend and still doing everything to protect the Colony, Jefferson and Madison still openly defend Adams's actions. While amongst themselves their faith in him has taken a steep downward spiral.

About this time, Soros and Nero have returned, with a couple of new rodents, Gaius and Reid, accompanying them. Both have the colorations and markings of 'Wilds,' and Gaius doesn't waste anytime in making his opinions about the 'Rodent Leader's' actions known. He openly criticizes Adams, saying that he's violated the 'Rodent Life Document' and should face disciplinary actions. With the help of Soros and Nero, he helps organize companies and alliances to attack Adams and the other 'Originals.' Soros and his allies spend their time trying to enlist support for the endeavor to have Adams removed from office.

Soros was even quoted as saying he would use all his resources to make sure he would not have a second term. This is all done in vain however, because Adams does win a second term, beating out the 'Hoarders' favorite Caesar by a large margin. Not as large as his first election, but still a large margin.

The agenda of the Hoarders is not without an amount of

success. Gaius' success at organizing rodents and other activities makes him a consideration for a candidate for a Senator. He wins this easily.

Adams' second term is for the most part more the same policies, the biggest changes are within the senate. The rodents make their frustration with Adams' policies clear by voting out many of the 'Originals,' in the senate and replacing them with 'Hoarders' instead. In an effort to move forward from this and unite the Colony, Adams kowtows to the whims of the demands of the opposing 'Group.' Despite this act of pacification the rewards of his efforts only gets him grief by them, being criticized worse than ever by the 'Hoarders.'

To make matters worse one of his staff gets a charge of ethics violation against him and the 'Rodent Leader' calls for 'Immunity from Charge' for him. The loudest voice in opposition is the newest and youngest senator, Gaius. Calling out Adams, saying he's violating our laws and shouldn't be interfering in the proceeding investigation by coddling one of his staff.

"If this were you or I, we would be held up for trial on these charges. Since it is a representative of the 'Rodent Leader,' he gets a free pass," Gaius claims. "That's not right and it's definitely not fair. I was under the impression that that was what these laws were supposed to do. Create not just freedom, but also equality for all, not just some."

His monologue has it's intended effect from the crowd and it only helps him in making a name and reputation for himself.

41

The goal of which is not entirely clear.

"He's up to something. They all are.." Jefferson says to the 'Rodent Leader' in their first meeting since his return to Colony.

"Who? What are they up? You mean like a conspiracy?" Adams asks.

"For the sake of argument; yes, like a conspiracy. I don't know who it is exactly or their plans. I guarantee that Gaius, Nero, and Soros are all involved somehow though."

"Do you have anything to back up that claim?"

"No... Mr. 'Rodent Leader.' I don't, I just know they are up to something and it can't be good."

"Okay. He's conspiring against us and all we stand for. What can we do about it... I'll tell you what, nothing. All you have is a hunch Jefferson, and you know myself or the Senate can't act on just a hunch."

"You have before, in the name of 'Colony Security.' What's stopping you now?"

"Yes, Jefferson I did, and as I recall you were adamantly opposed to that, were you not? That was different though, I can't go after a Senator without some validation. Don't condemn me for not breaking the laws that you yourself helped establish."

"I get your point. I'm also glad to hear you talk that way, that is the rat that I stood behind when you first started campaigning."

"Well, my campaign is coming to an end and you boys better get to work finding your next candidate. I hear that this

42

rat, Gaius, is going to be running and he's got a lot of resources and connections."

"Oh.. Like, who is on his side?"

"You mean besides, Soros, Caesar, and Nero? He also, has Clinton, Kerry, Shakespeare, and pretty much all of the 'Hoarders', as well as quite of few of the other 'Groups' and other activists backing him."

"Really….."

Adams' second term passes without any more major controversy, and with one major regret.. That the squirrel in charge of the destruction of the back end of the Colony, was not brought to justice. As for the former leader of the Manhattan Colony himself, he's decided to enjoy a retirement from 'Rodent -ment' and indulge in being a normal citizen again.

Now the Colony is going into its third election, it's between an older, cantankerous, war veteran, Cane and the young, charismatic, newcomer, Gaius. That's the image that the staff of Gaius are eagerly and effectively manipulating, in any case.

Jefferson is more anxious than ever with this election. Not because of what is known about Senator Gaius but because very little is known about him.

It's known that he is definitely a 'Hoarder' and sticks to their policies very rigidly. He claims to be a 'Domestie' as well, but his coloration looks more like a 'Wild.' There's something about him, that Jefferson can't put his claw on, leaving his feeling unsettled. He says just the right thing to just the right crowd, making promises that he can't keep without breaking them to another gathering. A few of the promises are too extreme, that he can't possibly deliver at all. What will happen when the rodents of the Manhattan Colony figure this out? Will there be mass hysteria? Looting? Murders? Suicides? Maybe worse, they won't react at all. Have they already reached that jaded apathy that their human cohabitants have excel in? Which would be worse?... The sudden appearance and popularity of such a mysterious rodent is most definitely troubling to Jefferson.

More troubling still, is the rodents he has connections with.

Soros, Nero, and Caesar, as well as the 'Alliances' bosses. The 'Alliances' are basically just industrial bullies after all, extorting from the those who they are supposed to be protecting. No, this newcomer is not a good omen..

Worse yet in the campaign is the rhetoric by Cane. Demonizing Adams, as much as Gaius does, trying in an effort to gain favor with the crowds by distancing himself from the former 'Rodent Leader.' But looking instead, like he is distancing himself from the 'Originals.' This has only been compounded by his actions as a Senator and making deals and getting a little too chummy with the 'Hoarders.' Things are looking bleak for the outcome of the Colony.

Then it happens. In the middle of hobnobbing with the crowd during the campaign, Gaius lets it slip out. "I'm going to Redistribute Food supplies." The words that Jefferson and the other more practical rats were waiting in horror to hear. This announcement sends a cold shiver down the rat's spine and he makes sure that as many of his fellow rodents knows about this as he can.

"So what? What's so bad about that?" asks one of the rats in the audience.

"What is wrong with that is the precedence it sets. He just admitted that he wants to take control of your lives, that's what's wrong with that. He wants a despotic government to be substituted into this free society that we have been working towards. Do you instead want to be a parasite? That's what he is saying that he wants from you, to become a blood-sucking tick, to the working rodent," Jefferson answers.

"It only hurts those with a lot of food stocks though. So why should we care about it? They don't care about me, and they haven't done anything to help me, right?" asks another member of the crowd.

This time Trump answers. "Those with food reserves are the ones who create industry, create jobs, hire rodents. Not only do they provide employment, but they also make the products that benefit every rodent in the Colony. Don't buy into the rancor of this creature of chaos. He wants to divide us and start a war between the have and have-nots. 'All for the good of the Colony' don't take his bait."

"You're one of them, of course you'd say that," responses a member of the crowd.

"How about me?" Jefferson asks, "do you have such

animosity towards me, the co-founder of the Colony? I wrote many of the laws that protect you and will protect your rodent -lings in the future. Do you feel that I'm a selfish rodent, looking out only for himself?" The crowd is silent. "I've known Trump for awhile now, he doesn't mince words, and he can be cold in his business dealings. That's how you have to be in business though, because it's cut throat and the pressures to improve the product and its process are always advancing. It's a race to the finish line. He has to make tough choices and sometimes it hurts rodents who work for him. In the end, it winds up being the best for all involved, those that are left get more time to work and more benefits. Those that leave more times than not get something better. The rest of society benefits from the advancement because we get a better product, for less resources. Everybody wins except for the 'Alliances' and the Senators, that's why Gaius wants to convince you that someone in this industrial love triangle is losing. He wants to get in to shake things up."

"Rodents like Trump have so much though. It just doesn't seem fair," says another rodent in the crowd breaking the silence.

"Equality is something that we have to make for ourselves, not have it dished out by those who make the laws. That's a fake equality, and it will inevitably shatter. Besides, do you really feel that taking from one rodent and giving to another is an ethical practice? No, of course it's not, but that's what he wants you to believe. Remember that there are rodents in a lower positions of society than you, how would you feel if this practice

was performed on you? Before you fall too deep into the trap
this serpent Gaius set, take that into consideration. Thank you,
my fellow rodents. Good day."

With that Jefferson turns and walks away, letting his
statement sink in. Some of the rodents are mulling this over,
while many still have not been convinced by the speech of their
society's founder. The effect of his words having no noticeable
dent on the consciousness of his audience. Jefferson has not
given up on the crowd and still hopes that they will do what is
best for all, for now that is all he can do.

But all his efforts are in vain in the end, the Gaius machine
is too big and powerful. Two grueling months later, Gaius is
elected 'Rodent Leader' of the Manhattan Colony.

CHAPTER FIVE:

THE COUP

The atmosphere in the Colony is an odd mixture of
unadulterated jubilance and total panic, with only a few rodents
not picking a side. Even those with animosity for the
'Hoarders' and the 'Originals' both join in their battle of
dominance. This should not a big surprise however, because
chaos was running rampant through the whole campaign. Voter
fraud and intimidation were reported across the Colony. There
were incidents of violence perpetrated against those who made
declarations of opposition to Gaius; these incidents were largely
ignored and even oppressed at times by the 'Rodent Security
Force.' This security squad is supposed to be an impartial
organization but their actions throughout has led to question
that assumption.

One report was that a Gaius supporter ran down a female
rodent and her rat-lings because she was wearing a Cane patch
on her dress. This was one encounter when the RSF did
intervene and he was charged.

Destruction of property by Gaius supporters have become common and accepted with the few incidents that Cane supporters treated as acts of treason. Not to try to validate their actions but some consistency of the law is needed and apparently absent.

Even many of the representatives of the rodent capitals are nervous about making any statements against the Senator. Some have had death threats made against them.

One of the oddest things is the sudden appearance of a Hawk that patrols the Colony. There have been increasing attacks on the residents while foraging, one of the Senators is even killed, under suspicious circumstances. All opponents of Gaius.

These threats are not going to scare Jefferson from his normal routines; even his regular outings to explore the perimeter of the Colony and to secure her best interests within the surrounding rodent communities. Jefferson, not being a foolish rat, though takes his proper precautions with the increased need of personal security. In time, these actions prove not to be a waste.

A couple of months before the election, while on his way to a meeting with one of the Upper end Squirrel ambassadors, Jefferson sees a large shadow circling overhead. This has gotten his guard up more than normal and not accepting the 'Political Security Services' protection, his alertness is definitely appropriate. Not seeing the exact location of the bird of prey, going back to the Colony strikes him as pointless, so the rat continues on his way. He does stop every couple of feet in his trek to check for anything that draws the attention of his senses. After awhile of no longer seeing the shadow he picks up his pace to what it was and is again making time to the meeting. Not knowing that the bird is perched on a branch in the tree right in front of him, poised and ready for the kill! A little closer… A little more… One more foot, the bird thinks to himself keeping his eyes unwaveringly focused on his target. He makes his strike, with eager anticipation he lowers his talons and fixes them into the strike position.

Before Jefferson knows what has happened he finds himself in the air, he first tries to reach his attacker's foot, without success. He then pulls out his concealed weapon, under his suit on his back he had hidden a human sewing pin. He shoves the needle deep into the bird's foot, the bird releases him. Jefferson fortunately had his tail wrapped in the eye of the needle and he forces his body into the air, leaping onto the hawk's back. Then using his suit jacket he blinds the bird, forcing him into a nearby tree.

In the process Jefferson breaks his shoulder and gets a few scrapes and bruises, but he does survive. The hawk is not so lucky and breaks his neck when he crashes into the trunk.

At the office of the Squirrel Ambassador, the Ambassador is getting impatient. "Where is Jefferson? You told me he was on his way, it should not have taken him this long!"

"I don't know sire. I will send out a message with the royal sparrow to find out," replies the Ambassador's assistant.

"Don't bother!" comes a voice from the entryway. It is the disheveled and uncharacteristically late Jefferson.

As he gets into closer view, the Ambassador's anger
melts into concern seeing the condition of his guest.

"Jefferson. My Comrade, what has happened to you?"

"Nothing too exciting, just a fight with a precocious bird
of prey. It looks worse than it is."

"Still, I think my medical officers should look you over.
I insist."

"Normally I would argue with you, but today I think I
will consider that counsel."

"Was it that same hawk patrolling the area?"

"It's been here too, huh? Yes, the same one. It won't
be anymore."

"Oh?" the Ambassador asks.

"We kind of crashed into a tree and let's just say the tree
won. It broke its neck during the accident. I'll tell you
something, I don't think its presence is a coincidence either, I
think someone made a deal with it to eliminate their political
threats…. Like some kind of assassin."

"Who sent it? Do you know?" the Ambassador whispers
to Jefferson.

"Not for certain, but I have my suspicions. If I can
confirm them, I will make sure they face justice for these acts
of tyranny. That is a promise."

The rest of his visit with the Ambassador was uneventful,
they discussed their issues and worked on resolutions, had
dinner, met with other officials including a first meeting with
the Chipmunks Ambassador. Jefferson spent the night at the
Squirrel's Colony and spent another day there to wrap up the

51

rest of their business. The next day he left for the comforts of his own home. A fire different from any other was burning inside his heart and his head, one that could only be put out with the defeat of this newcomer, Gaius. This is a future that Jefferson will never know however.

His first day back, Jefferson calls a press conference; during this conference he speaks in rare form even for him! With a calm demeanor and a resolute tone echoing in his voice he delivers his greatest speech, offering up all the reasons that this brash and impetuous Gaius has no right to the office he covets and no ability to be an effective 'Rodent Leader.' His speech is indeed effective and gains the attention of Gibbs and Reid, two particularly devious rats and assistants to Gaius. After the speech they report to Gaius.

Gaius was already livid about Jefferson's miraculous survival of the encounter with the hawk.

"We must finish this Jefferson. He is the only force that we cannot neutralize. He has to go," Gaius tells he cohorts.

"We will plan an accident," Gibbs offers.

"Sounds good. Have him followed and look for opportunities."

"I'll send my best rodent," says Gibbs, with a sneer.

He doesn't have to wait long for his chance, when news is reported that Jefferson is going to the library to reference notes on International Relations.
A couple of days before the trek, the rodent sent to kill Jefferson goes to the library to set the trap for the Statesrat.

"Hello, Gorby, how are you my friend?"

"Good and you? You're here early, the library is still open," Gorby answers back.

"Good as well. I know and I apologize for that, but I don't have any other time to come in. Have you been keeping up on your studies during my absence?"

"Well I guess I can let it slip this one time, and indeed I have. I just finished *The Art of War.*"

"That's an excellent book. Do you have anything good about international relations? I have a meeting with the Chipmunk Ambassador next week and need to study up."

"Well let's see," Gorby replies, heading to the computer. As well as learning to read he has learned the library computer system. He types in the topic in the search box and the two look for the results in the stacks of books.

Making sure to stay out of sight Jefferson finds a dark out of the way place to study on the upstairs floor. He spends a couple of hours studying the books, making notes about certain points for memory. He wraps up his studies and stretches. When he does he sees something that catches his eye. A book on the Roman Empire, he had always been curious about why the name Gaius sounded familiar. He hops over to the table that the book is resting and drags it to his study spot. He looks the book over searching for the name. He finally finds it and shudders, putting his paws to his mouth. "It can't be him…" Jefferson replies, then considers his finding. "It does make sense though." Jefferson slams the book shut in disgust and heads down to see Gorby who has stayed upstairs to help him.

"Gorby, I must go! I have to figure out a way to stop

Gaius from winning the election.." At this point, his discovery is not the only surprise the rat will receive this night.

"What? What is it?" Gorby asks.

"I think that's Becky and her parents," Jefferson answers.

"Who?" Gorby asks.

"Sorry, my former owners. What a weird coincidence for them to be here."

But he does not have a chance to ponder this over for long, because the building shakes and fills with smoke. In the commotion, Jefferson disappears from Gorby's sight. The floor caves in and Gorby disappears with it. Jefferson is trying to get back to the cat but the last thing that he sees is a brick from the ceiling that falls his way.

Madison is at a meeting with the other 'Originals,' when his assistant runs in, clearly shaken and out of breath.

"Tony! What is it? Here have some water and collect yourself."

After a couple of deep breaths and a cup of water the rat is able to articulate. "Okay.. Now what is it, Tony?"

"It's…. Statesrat Jefferson. He was at the library, and there was an accident," Tony reports in a shaky voice.

"What do mean an accident?.. What kind of accident?… Is he alright?" Madison, pressing his assistant, pulling him away from the rest of the crowd.

"There was an explosion… Jefferson… He didn't make it. He's dead."

"Are you serious? Jefferson is DEAD!!" Madison, almost screams the last part. He lies down and holds his hands to his

54

eyes, and lets a few tears slip through before he draws in a deep breath to compose himself.

He starts to stand up and his assistant helps him the rest of the way, not letting go until he's sure Madison can hold his own weight.

"I'll be okay now. Thank you, Tony."

"Of course. What do you want me to do? Should I tell the rest of the guests?" Tony, asks.

"Um… No, I'll go tell them. You can go home for the night."

"Yes sir. If you need anything, let me know."

"Thank you, Tony."

Madison takes a couple of minutes and another deep breath, before heading back in to join the rest of them. When he goes inside the first thing he does is grab a drink, then he gets to his very unpleasant announcement.

"Excuse me everyone, I have some very terrible news. As you may have heard, Statesrat Jefferson went on an information scouting mission to the library. While there, the building exploded and… Jefferson was killed."

Like a balloon being deflated, the crowd instantly stops conversing and the only sounds are that of grasps and sobs. The last barrier for Gaius' victory is gone, two weeks later he is inaugurated 'Rodent Leader.'

CHAPTER SIX:

INSANITY REIGNS

The expectations that the new 'Rodent Leader'
have set for himself are quite high, but if he's worried it doesn't
show. He has said during his campaign that he will unite the
Colony and create the level of harmony that even Jefferson
never dreamed of and even he would have approved of Gaius'
policies for the end results. That's Gaius alright, always ready
with the right thing to say. The biggest problem is that none of
it is true. To start off with, he has not united the Colony but
made it more divided than ever. Starting with his class warfare
tactics, citing the Working Rodents as the causes of all the
Colony's woes, leaving those without in the cold and not giving
them the opportunities to advance in the Colony. He doesn't
mention that all the rodents in the Colony have had the same
opportunities as they have; but let's face it, that's not practical

propaganda.

A month before the elections, there was a crash in the 'Dwellings' market and the 'Food Stock Systems' needed government assistance. The 'Working Rodents' government payments of food stocks were given to them to repair the damage. One of many things that should have been questioned is the conflict of interest of loaning it to Frank, a cohort of Gaius. But the citizens thought that government loan was the best option for the given situation, unfortunately this is only the first of many loans to come and many very questionable. Most of these are ones that lean towards Gaius' causes and have not improved their condition with the additional funding. More than a couple have in fact gone under. Rather than let the companies sort it out and eliminate waste and inefficiency, the companies are given a pass and free food stocks are now how all such situations are handled. All the industries that fight against the new policies are demonized by the 'Rodent Leader.' The government buy out of all the most profitable private industries has begun. Another related buyout is using 'Working Rodent' payments to buy up depreciated dwellings.

Whenever Gaius is questioned about it he just goes into a speech about it's all done in the name of fairness and equality and diverts attention from the issue.

That and blaming the previous 'Rodent Leader' which is a tactic that he uses throughout his first term no, matter how feeble that declaration might be. When the downfall of the prosperity in the Colony happens because of the 'Food Stocks System Scandal' it is of course because of the Adams' giving breaks to the well to do Rodents, like Trump and the other 'Industrials.' It couldn't be because of his using the Food Stocks as his own personal credit account.

The main platform Gaius runs under is one of 'Rodent -ment' promised healthcare. It's an enormous bill that doesn't fix the problems that it says it does and the ones mentioned by the 'Rodent Leader' are already commonly provided by many healthcare 'Assurance' providers, such as rodent-lings up to t wenty six months will still be covered by their parents 'Assurance' package. Or that already diagnosed aliments will still receive care. Both are already provided by the companies, they just had to shop around to find them. Its entire justification is made by the 'Speaker Rodent' Pelousy (when she was deciding her name she misheard someone pronouncing the name and didn't get the joke. Not wanting to admit the error she keep the name as is).

"We have to get it signed before you can read it. You can't know what is in it," Pelousy was reported to have said.

"Speaker Pe-Lousy," Madison, purposely emphasizes before asking his question, "If YOU don't know what was written, then WHO does? Didn't YOU write it?"

"Statesrat Madison, I know what is in it, but we have to pass it before we can present it to the Citizens."

Pelousy seems completely oblivious to it, but she made a very chilling comment, saying that it can't be seen by the populace before hand and that was all that Madison wanted to hear.

Gaius-care is just one more industry being purchased by

58

the Gaius Administration using food stocks.

In the campaign another promise made by Gaius was that he would end the Low Ender War with the Squirrels, within the first year of his term, as well as closing 'Gitmore' a prisoner detention center for the 'Rodents Of War.' Because of lack of support and funding by the senators that was put on the backburner and didn't happen until the end of his second year, with the exception of 'Gitmore', it was never closed. The accusations of extreme torture of ROW's was not confirmed and it was written off as just a witch hunt against Adams' Lower End War. This is made more obvious when he increases the insurgents in the far end of the park against the Chipmunks and starts another engagement against the Squirrels in the Riverside Park. The reasons for these actions are not really clear.

Many of his other bills and laws are just extensions of those already in existence. Funding on agendas that the Rodents of the Colony found controversial is the norm under Gaius and the great uniter is dividing the Colony more and more everyday. It's basically like Christmas morning for the most outrageous in the Colony and they protect him ferociously claiming that those who accuse him of any wrongdoing are 'Domesties' and just uncomfortable about a 'Wild' for their 'Rodent Leader.' Many rodents including 'Domesties' have flocked to the Colony so this claim has some possible backing, but that does not explain away the ridicule by rodents like Madison. Their condemnation of Gaius and his policies are explained as being traitors to their race. Being that Gaius claims to be half 'Domestie,' this is really an odd statement if

59

examined carefully. One of the policies is an extension on the already existing anti-bigotry laws. Another is one written to protect the rights of choice for a expectant female rodent to be able to have an unwanted rodent-ling prematurely born and left to die, all paid for by the 'Working Rodent's' 'Rodent-ment' Payments.

Also troubling is the methods he uses to sidestep the Senators rulings on issues, being a well educated rat having studied rodent laws thoroughly, he's using the loopholes to get his way. One of which he uses that gets his cohorts into positions of power as heads of departments. While not illegal, it does make sure that they are not possibly denied these positions by the Senators who are the ones who normally would make the final decisions after careful deliberation and discussions. This way they get in without any senatorial judgment. He also gets to appoint two new judges, one is a chipmunk activist who has strong leanings towards eliminating the rules for migrating rodents and the other a rat who wants to take away all rodent rights to self preservation. Just the kind of rodents that Gaius loves to surround himself with.

The only commendable act performed by Gaius is the repeal of 'The No Rodent-ling Left Behind,' but this is only a partial repeal offered to the parts of the Colony with large support for him and his 'Educational Alliance' bosses. Reports have been coming in of his interference in the educational system, having the students being raised with songs praising Gaius, instead of the traditional ones showing pride for the Colony.

In another spending project he puts excessive food stock into roads and dwellings maintenance, whether it's needed or not.

Gaius now owns most of the industrial, educational, food stock, and healthcare programs in the Colony and has outspent Adams by more than double. All this without a reported budget for the Senators to approve of.

These are just the problems that his empirical policies has created, that doesn't even cover his other bad decisions. A company that brings drinking water into the Colony has a line break and a flood starts. What does the 'Rodent Leader' do first. Go to the site and help out?.. Send his staff familiar with the company in to investigate? None of the above, he makes a statement condemning the company for negligence and blames the 'Originals.' Madison, fuming from this and not intending to sit by the sidelines makes a scathing retort in a press statement critical of Gaius' actions.

"We need leadership from the 'Rodent Leader' at a time like this," states Madison, in part of the reported statement. "Instead we get demagoguery of the 'Originals.' Typical, for this 'Rodent Leader.'"

For over a month, Gaius does nothing to help the situation and instead continues trashing the company, and trying to get the penalties for the spill increased. All the while the company involved are fixing the situation, suffering great expense and being ridiculed by Gaius supporters.

He introduces a bill to generate more openness in the politicians, at a time when he himself is being more closed about his past, with inconsistencies in the story of his life.

Also very distressing for the 'Originals' is how he spends 'Working Rodent' payments without any real thought of the ethical considerations of it. He spent many 'Food Stocks' on vacations out of the Colony, the finest meals, and other such extravagances, then he condemns the 'Industrial Rodents' for doing the same with their hard earned food stocks. When he celebrates the holidays and his rat-lings birthdays with his celebrity rodent friends, like Shakespeare, they throw elaborate parties. Out in public he puts on an even bigger show than his entertainer supporters, singing, going to sporting events, bars, and other activities that are beneath the office of 'Rodent Leader.'

In an odd act, he goes to the other parts of the park that have always been hostile towards the Colony and apologizes to them for the actions of the Colony to them. To the Colony's allies, he goes on the warpath, seemingly intentionally antagonizing them and making their lives a living hell. Accomplishing all of this before the end of his first term.

The end of Gaius' first term is coming up now and the elections are almost here again. It's between Gaius and a Industrial Rodent named Bain. Bain was a candidate in the last election that got pushed out by Cane and another possible 'Rodent Leader.'

What he went through last time has prepared him for this run, though and if he can survive the onslaught from his fellow 'Originals,' then he might be able to handle Gaius. Another couple of candidates, Newt and Sanatorium, both establishment 'Originals' are the major causes of Bain's woes. But that is just their patterns, seeing as they are sniping at all the others in the race. The number starting out is very large at seven, but quickly dwindles down to four by the end. Being in the business field and helping others start theirs through a lending company that he worked for, he has held tough and wins the 'Originals' nomination for 'Rodent Leader.' Going by the standard set by the 'Originals' debates, many of the press is predicting that the 'Originals'/ 'Hoarders' debate will be the worst ever.

Gaius has had some problems in this campaign that he didn't have last time, for one thing... resources. Through stupid mistakes Gaius' has lost a lot of the support that he had won with last time.

The youth rodent vote for starters, many of them voted for him because he talked a good talk and made a lot of promises. Most of them he did deliver on. However, they just didn't know the repercussions of them. The biggest side effect, job loss. Under Gaius' watch, the unemployment doubled and many professional rodents had to take the less illustrious jobs that the rodent-lings needed. That was the cause and effect of the Gaius economy and it was a hard learned lesson indeed.

Another demographic effected by this is the rodent

63

minorities, mice, squirrels, and chipmunks, who came from the Riverside park to escape the oppressive Squirrels. They also take the menial jobs as well and the benefits provided by Gaius doesn't make up for this in the minds of many of them. Trying to rally their support, he fights for them under the claim of voter laws that are aimed at discouraging their voting, saying they are full of bigotry for asking them for identification.

Another blunder made by Gaius is his stance on same gender weddings, making them legal and alienating the 'Wilds' who find this practice unnatural.

Then there are the questionable actions taken by his government representatives. Scandals with the 'Political Security Services' and the 'Rodent Information Agency,' keeping company with prostitutes while out of the Colony, where it's not illegal. For them it still is; being representatives of the Colony and all. Another scandal involves the 'Main Officer,' an especially devious rat named Holder. Holder is accused of having knowledge of a number of weapons going across the Colony border and a 'Rodent Security Force' officer losing his life in the scandal.

When asked for all the information on the events, he refuses, with contempt charges being lead by the 'Originals' against him. These charges are never approved and Gaius calls "Immunity from Charge" for his 'Main Officer.' A sorry spectacle for the 'Rodent Leader' and makes rodents wonder, is this a showing of what is left to happen under Gaius' watch?

All that aside, Gaius isn't too worried about going against Bain, mostly for one big reason, he doesn't have a problem lying

to serve his purpose. That's what he does and very well too.
Bain's charges against Gaius might be exaggerations but at least
there is some truth in what he says. Gaius just makes things up.

Since the ending of the Lower Ender War about the
middle of his second year, there have been extra Drones,
dragonflies trained for surveillance and to attack rodents
suspected of terror-rodent activities. Rodents leaving the
Colony have been subjected to intrusive searches, because of
kamikaze terror-rodents who have snuck explosive devices in
themselves and into travel areas of the Colony. More of a
concern than anything else is the announcement of a 'Kill List'
that the 'Rodent Leader' has written up, at the moment it has
mostly terror-rodent threats but the implications made of this
revelation gives hints to a future one that will cover all who
question him, including the Colony's own residents.

The things that have gone right in the Colony, he is all too
eager to take credit for, even if his actions had in fact made the
situation into the calamity in the first place. For example, the
hard times in the Colony had all the evidence pointing to his
intervening in it, yet he takes credit for the dismal and timid
recovery. If not for his actions, it would have been a stronger
and faster recovery. During his time as 'Rodent Leader' he had
had the success of military missions, with the removal of more
than a few of the most dangerous terror-rodents including Laden,
the one responsible for the great destruction of the back end of
the cavern. The disgusting things about the whole affair is that
he takes the credit for its success and not giving it to the
Solider-rodents.

A common attitude in the Colony amongst those still supporting the 'Rodent Leader,' is that he hasn't had enough time, to implement his ideas, that is something that should cause exaltation in the whole Colony, but the worst is sure to come.

CHAPTER SEVEN:

REVOLUTION

It was a lingering and brutal election with a most

disheartening outcome; while it was close all the way, with claims

that both voter intimidation and voter fraud have increased, by

the 'Hoarders,' Gaius is reelected for a second term.

The major reason for this outcome has to do with the

corruption of the judicial system. Time and time again, the

judges avoid all reason and side with the 'Rodent Leader,' not

wanting to look bad with him because of their perceived exulted

status of Gaius, they basically just gave him the office. Instead

of the Rodents deciding their fate, it is in the hands of the

judges.

Now that he doesn't have to be hindered by the opinion

of the rodent citizens at all, he doesn't waste any time

eliminating the 'Rodent's Rights.'

First, as predicted he expands the 'Kill List,' to include

any rodent who has been critical of the 'Rodent Leader.' The

list now has the names of most of the senators and the rodent citizens. Before they can be tracked down and hanged, Madison and the Statesrats and Senators flee.

The 'Originals' who do stay behind are either coerced into abandoning their 'group' and swear allegiance, those who do neither are sent to the gallows. The only living opposition to Gaius is now in exile. The 'Rodent Leader' who was supposed to bring all rodents together, to bring hope and prosperity to all Rodent-kind has killed every shred of hope.

He then transforms the 'food stock' system into the 'food ration plan,' making it so that food is no longer used as currency.
His rationale is that since the government owns all the food anyways, it only makes sense that it is rationed out. Now the barter system is dead and all resources are in the hands of Gaius and his advisers.

With the Senators and Statesrats out of the way he goes about starting the next part of his plan, the complete dismantling of the 'Rodent's Rights.' The drones are now increased and circle the underground cities, constantly, watching and preying on the residents. The RSF has been increased to massive levels and a new Squirrel Army is created as well. New laws are written daily and the old ones are rendered obsolete. 'Alliance' bosses rule the industries, Gaius propaganda is everywhere, the press only now talks about traitors to Gaius and his 'Rodentopia' vision. The Squirrel Army and the RSF patrol the pathways in the Colony and a curfew is put into place that is strictly enforced. The authority of these forces are now absolute and the 'Rodent's Rights' no longer exist.

Departments are now formed to head up and maintain the new social standards by Gaius and his regime. Head of Food Stocks, Head of Resources, Head of Working Rodents Issues, Working Rodents Alliance, Head of Health and Rodent Services, Head of Capital Punishment, Head of Rodent Justice, for every aspect of rodent life there is now a department for it.

The Industrial Rodents follow the lead of the Senators and flee the Colony, not because their lives are in jeopardy though, but because of the even more increased regulations placed on them. It is no longer profitable to set up an enterprise there.

A new turn of propaganda has been spearheaded by the newly born 'Propaganda Committee'; with the rodent threats gone Gaius' new target is the humans. With fierce tenacity they strike, making sure every last rodent has gotten the word, that humans are our enemy and they must be neutralized...
The Human Genocide has begun.

"We must take this to the streets and do to them as they have done to us for many generations. Poisons, traps, violent attacks against them, it doesn't matter how we do it. As long as the humans positions over us and all Animal kind are lost . I say to you on this day, the worst vermin doesn't scurry about in fur or take flight in feathers, but in fact walk on two legs and wear the garments created from the hides or fur of the Animal Kingdom. We the rodents, must do what is needed today. We must eliminate this threat to our way of life. Long live the Manhattan Colony." From the crowd comes an eruption of celebration, like the trained rodents that they are.

69

Rather than hide from the humans and sneak food from their refuse, now an all out assault has been set to take it from them. When it first begins it is simply theft of their food and 'Do Not Feed the Wildlife' signs are posted in response. Thinking that will be the end of it, what happens next is completely unexpected. One of Gaius' staff went through and marked the sign in green paint with the words, 'WE THE RODENTS.' Some humans are savagely brutalized and need to be hospitalized because of blood loss and trauma; others from bouts of Rabies and other ailments transmitted by the rodents. The rodents may have made the initial blow but they will not win and the humans strike back, eradicating every rat, squirrel, and chipmunk on first sight. This only enrages Gaius more and he calls for further violence and calculated strategic military engagements for the Squirrel Army and the RSF. Despite his claim to the contrary, he institutes a Draft and all able bodied rodents are initiated into his war with the humans. While this action has further disenfranchised the rodents of the Colony, they dare not speak up.

One outspoken member of the rodent press does write an article calling for restraint, in part it read: 'In our past, many generations ago our race killed many humans in a revolution that the humans called 'The Black Plague.' It was considered nothing more than a dark day in their history and not the early attempt at their eradication we know it to be.

I would rather be a vermin who with the absence of malice kills hundreds of thousands of another race (the humans), than be a rodent of unprecedented and total power, and murder or enslave millions of any other race, including the humans. Gaius' call for dominance over them has no validation and is a crime against nature itself. This is a claim of rodent superiority, it is 'Rodent-ism,' and it is wrong plain and simple.' The author of this article is never heard from again.

Despite all this, the citizens stand behind Gaius, believing that he still has their best interests at heart. He pacifies them with statements, much as he did before, only now claiming that the founder Jefferson would have approved his measures, though extreme, because of the end results.

"I do all this to help out my fellow rodent, rat, chipmunk, squirrel, mouse, we are all in this together and must remain united as one force. We must win this Rodent Revolution. Together there is nothing we can't accomplish, we can have a fair and just society, we just need to make it. Together we can," Gaius says in a speech, reports a member of the press.

"Amazing, absolutely miraculous. Its commanding and rousing dialect like that that reminds us of why Gaius is so great a Rodent Leader. No one since Jefferson has ever been so inspirational," the reporter gushes. Apparently propaganda can create pseudo collaboration in any society, human or animal.

CHAPTER EIGHT:

SECRETS REVEALED

Outside of the Colony, things are back to the old

ways of survival for the banished Senators, 'Statesrats,' and 'Industrial' rodents. Most have been sticking together for mutual support and have formed a semi-communal structure. But Madison has been keeping to himself lately. He, unlike most of the others, has not given up on their Manhattan Colony, but feels that it is best not only for himself, but for the Colony to remain in exile. So he waits for his chance to return.

Trump too, has not given up and the two of them talk about their future plans to bring sanity back to their home.

A couple of months after their banishment that day comes, in the most unexpected form... Nero.

"Madison?" Nero calls out from the shadow where Madison is foraging.

"Nero! Shouldn't you be groveling to your god of destruction? What do you want, to see me under the cover of desperation? If that's it then go, because I won't give you the satisfaction," Madison snarls at the intruder.

"SHHH! I can't be seen here, but I have something to talk to you about. Meet me at the remains of the library at midnight alone. I have something that you will want to hear."

"Why should I possibly trust you?"

Nero sighs before answering. "Because I think you, Jefferson, and the rest of the 'Originals,' were, at least partially right and I found something interesting. Think about it, I'm here risking my life. If nothing else doesn't that make you curious." A noise behind them makes Madison turn away from Nero. It was just a piece of paper floating in the wind. When he turns back, Nero is gone.

Madison has been pacing nervously around the burnt hallways for the past twenty minutes. Always early as is his custom, he can't settle down while he waits for Nero. He's not all that anxious about the rendezvous, as much as the location. A cold chill goes up and down the rat's back as he walks the corridors, hearing the screams of the victims, feeling their ghosts haunting him. He turns to go down a hallway and sees a familiar face, his mentor and friend, Jefferson. He goes to greet him, finding himself face to face with Nero. His excitement turns to disgust and he turns away from Nero.

"Madison, I'm sorry about what happened here, I really am. Believe it or not I had a lot of admiration for Jefferson and felt nothing but sorrow for his loss."

"Look, I'm here. You said you had something for me. Let's get on with it so I can go."

"Okay, that's fair. I found this first off." He hands Madison a note with Jefferson's handwriting.

It read:

Becky,

Get out now. You're in danger!

"That doesn't make any sense! That would mean he already knew what was going to happen," Madison, exclaims.

"That's because he did," comes a booming voice behind them.

It was Gorby, who had snuck up behind Madison.

"Gorby! It is so good to see you! I thought the building had taken you as well," he says, and without a hesitation hugs one of the feline's legs. Gorby in turn returns the gesture with the other leg.

"I have something you must know, it has to do with that night," Gorby says, "Jefferson did find out what was going to happen a couple of minutes before and did all he could to help his former owners. I do think this was a trap set for him. It was too big of a coincidence, them being here."

"Who did it?" Madison asks.

"I don't know. There were some odd sounds and smells a

74

couple of nights before, but I found nothing."

"I did however, find something interesting," Nero chimes in, "What he was looking at that night."

Nero drags the book over to Madison. The Roman Emperors. Madison opens it and goes to the back of it, looking through the index.

He finds Gaius in it and turns to that page. There it was, the final nail in Jefferson's coffin, the bit of information that he couldn't have been allowed to live knowing. Gaius was the given name of one of the most sadistic and brutal emperors of ancient Rome… Caligula.

"That's why he had to go. Gaius knew that Jefferson would find this out. Not him.. This explains a lot though…"

"What do you mean?" Gorby asks.

"Rats in the Colony pick their own names. I never really understood the significance of it myself," Nero says.

"It gives a clue into the mindset of the rodent who picks it. That's why. If you pick like say, Gandhi or someone who did good, it shows who you really are. This is worse than I could have imagined. Caligula was one of the most detestable human beings on earth. He presented himself as a man of the people by humiliating the senators of Rome and spreading the class warfare myth. The ones who were looking out for the people were the senators, they tried to preserve the republic from his tyrannical hand. He took all the rights from the people of Rome by distracting them. Sound like anyone we know."

"Look, you and I don't see eye to eye on things but we do agree that Gaius has gone too far.."

"Caligula! Caligula has gone too far and he won't stop as long as he has power, because that is what he is addicted to.

That's what I have always been against, I don't care how he wants to live his life as long as he lets others decide their own fates."

"That's very eloquent, but it doesn't change things. I told you this so you can find a solution."

"My solution is to get justice for Jefferson, the Senators, the Statesrats, and the Colony as a whole. I am a representative of the rodent citizens of the Colony, not of the 'Originals.'"

"Then let's figure this out," Nero says.

"Here is my proposal then, we need to find a rodent who's neither an 'Original' or a 'Hoarder,' to replace Caligula. He won't listen to the will of the rodents and will continue to enslave them and wage war against the rest of the world. We will hold a special tribunal for him in the 'Working Rodent's' court. Let the common rodents decide his fate. Then we will bring out our candidates for them to decide."

"I don't get how that will change things?" Nero asks.

"Caligula has not hidden anything from the citizens this time, they know exactly who and what he is, he is a 'Rodent-ist.' He has crowned himself king over all. Besides, he has to face justice for what he did to Jefferson, the humans, the 'Industrials,' and the Senators."

"The humans, 'Industrials,' and the Senators! Why do they deserve justice? Look what they have done to their fellow rodents, leaving them in poverty, causing war…"

"Yes, and Caligula has fixed all that, hasn't he," Madison

interrupts Nero before he can get going into a tirade, and not intending it he goes into one himself. I'm getting tired of that song and dance. It's all the fault of those who have, keeping down those who have-not, it can't possibly be the individual themselves. Trump, Carnegie, Rockefeller, Bain, all these rodents were given such advantages. Wait a minute, but they weren't, they made hard choices and designed a superior product or service, or improved an existing one. It's far easier to take from them, than to try to be more like them. So let's leave the class warfare rhetoric at the door with Caligula, shall we!" Madison says. When he finishes, he's shaking with anger.

"Well this is very informative," Gorby interjects, "but I don't think this helps anything. What are you going to do?"

"The only way to defeat any army is with an army defending itself. The humans of this country won their freedom with militia and a band of rebels without real training and look what they have gained from it. That's what we need Gorby, will you help us?"

"Yes my little friend. I will be honored."

"Let's say we do all that," Nero says, "What the? We still have to prove that Gaius and his representatives caused Jefferson's death."

"We will figure that out when it happens, for now let's focus on getting together troops. Are you going to be able to go against Caligula and the 'Hoarders', if needs be?"

"I feel he has crossed a line, yes I can!" Nero replies.

"Then let's get our army."

CHAPTER NINE:

JUSTICE

With a gait of determination, Madison walks to

his destination of an alley nearby, he finds Trump and some of
the other industrials. He asked Trump to find as many of them
as he could, about ten of the fifteen of them showed up.

"All the ones I could find showed up," Trump says, with
anticipation.

"Good," Madison says, "we need all the help we can get.
I have come to find out that our 'Rodent Leader' is indeed a
cold blooded killer, before he even had the laughable and
ambiguous legal authority to assassinate his political enemies
under the 'Kill List,' he did so. The target in that case was our
Colony's own founder, Jefferson. The accident that ended is
life was not an accident at all, that part is something that is no
longer in dispute. We know it was an assassination, we just
can't prove it. He also has been hiding a large secret, for his
chosen identity of Gaius is the real name of Caligula and he is

apparently, just as despicable as his namesake, for intentionally deceiving us all. He must be removed from power if our civilization is to survive. That has become an undeniable truth now. We also have an unexpected ally in all of this, someone who has come forward at great personal risk and has provided as with this information and proof of a conspiracy. Nero, come out please."

Grumbling and murmurs follow Nero as he walks toward Madison at the front of the gathering. He glances nervously about the crowd, with indignation and hatred in their eyes. As an extra precaution, Gorby has been poised in a position behind Madison to act as crowd control. When he reaches Madison, the last rodent's scornful gaze he meets is Trump's.

"Jefferson was a very dear friend of mine and Nero here has earned my trust through his actions. I hope you will choose to do the same. Tell them."

Nero clears his throat and starts. "I found a note in Jefferson's handwriting, written the night of the explosion to his former owners who were also at the library. That's a very big coincidence in my opinion. Gorby has told us, that he was there, when there was some odd stirrings a couple of nights before the explosion. Jefferson discovered Gaius' true name of Caligula the night he died, and we have reason to believe he was going to tell the Colony this. He was already on the 'Kill List,' but if he was not, I do believe that that act would have put him on it.

Gaius has done some very atrocious things since your banishment, the Senators and Statesrats that stayed behind were

79

hanged, his judges now preside, and the 'Alliance' bosses control all industry. He is killing everything that Jefferson has worked for and has to be stopped. We might disagree on many things, but not that."

"Thank you, Nero. Now the way I see it we need to take things back from Caligula and put it back in the hands of the 'Working Rodents.' The first step is a showing of force, raise an army against his. Go into the streets talk to the urban rats, talk to the sparrows, the mice, each and every beast who will listen to our cause. They have been terrorized by Caligula and his forces as much as any, so I doubt it will be difficult getting recruits. Let's find them out. So for now I say, meeting adjourned."

So they go and spread out across the city searching out any animal that shows sympathy for their cause. Some join up because of the cause itself, others because they knew Jefferson and thought him to be a great rodent, then some joined because they had had run ins with Caligula and wanted him out of power.

The city rats were more than happy to oblige since Jefferson was known for his philanthropic endeavors with them, joining the effort in droves. There were even a couple of stray dogs and cats who even joined after hearing of his bravery. Between the despotism of Caligula and the gallantry of Jefferson, it was no time before they already have amassed a large resistance.

The next night there was one more meeting at the library. Madison steps up to address them.

"Many of you here know this, but for those new to the cause that don't, this is the site where we lost our society's founder, Jefferson. He was a remarkable rat, one of honor and a champion of liberty. He would have loved to know that just because he is no longer with us, the fire that he started in all of us has not gone out, but in fact has turned into an inferno. We will go to fight for the only cause that is really worth fighting for, freedom. We will not all live through the raid, but for those who don't while you might not have lived as free rodents or any other animal for that matter, you will have died as one. As for our non rodent brothers and sisters of the animal kingdom.. This is not your war, but you are putting yourselves in jeopardy anyways, I can't thank you enough for that. Let's take back the city, let's take back our lives, let's take back our freedom!"

That night the army starts it's trek to the Colony. Along the way the army unexpectedly keeps growing in size, some are just onlookers following the swarm to see what will happen. Most are part of the effort though. It takes a couple of days to reach their destination and they are greeted by a pair of RSF guards.

"Move along, Vermin. You have been banished and lost all your rights and privileges given by Gaius," says one of the guards. This comment makes Madison jump into action, literally. Madison tackles the squirrel and pins him to the ground, before he or the others can react. By the time the guards gain back their senses, both are disarmed and lying in the dirt.

"Move along, Vermin. MOVE ALONG, VERMIN.

After all I have done for you, that's the level of respect I get,
Move along Vermin. I was one of the founders of this Colony,
that you two cowards are helping to hold hostage. Jefferson
and I are the ones who wrote the laws that give you, Caligula, or
as you call him Gaius, and the rest of the Colony its rights and
privileges. Not some rodent dictator who is addicted to power
and knows the rodent laws. It's time that those in power give it
back to those who it really belongs to and I think we should
begin with the two of you."

That's when the rest of the army comes into the RSF
guard's view and they just look at each other helplessly, as the
resistance marches into the Colony. As they head into the city
they are shocked at the sight of how the Colony has changed
and not for the better. In the pathways armed RSF guards are
all over, propaganda about Gaius' greatness are all over, posters
with his face are as well. Announcements are made over a loud
speaker system that has been installed reminding its citizens of
the greatness of its 'Rodent Leader.' The citizens are seen
being harassed by RSF guards. 'Alliance' bosses are
everywhere.

Madison turns his head. A tear escapes from his eye, but
as can be seen from the facial expression on his face it's not
one of sorrow, and definitely, not one of joy. It's one of white
hot rage. He turns his head back his eyes filled with fury and he
turns back to face the army.

"We knew it would be bad and it won't be easy but this
is our home too. If we are unwilling to take it back and defend
it, we are not deserving of it. I would rather die a free rodent

than die Caligula's slave. This is not for me, or you, or Jefferson. This is for our future rodents, this is for liberty. This is for The Manhattan Colony."

This speech is met with calls of determination, in all the different vocalizations of the animal kingdom.

Their first strike is against the RSF harassing the rodents on the street, jumping the soldiers and knocking them down. They are then disarmed. Those who they rescue who don't join the fight are taken to safety. Those who do, join in the advancement. As they go further into the city, their ranks continue to swell as do their defensive provisions from the disarmed guards. Now an armada of venerable force, they head to the middle of the city and start purging the Colony of the detested despot. The posters, flags, and other such propaganda are set on fire. The statue of Caligula, in the city commons is wrapped with ropes and toppled. The rodent rebels continue their fight, as the RSF is sent out to try to contain them. But the rebels numbers are too large and they do little to break them as a force.

The Drones are sent in to assassinate the rebels, as are the other insect swarms. Many a rodent and insect die, but they press on. Hummingbirds are sent in to try to finish them off as well, they also inflict just a considerably small amount of damage to the rebel's numbers. The RSF have sent for reinforcements, only a couple of the birds sending the messages get through, most are killed by the stray dogs and cats. When the reinforcements do arrive the dogs and cats dispatch them before any can even get through the entrance. The dogs and cats are now being dive-bombed by the pigeons, but this is more of a nuisance than a real threat, and the cats take care of them. Now the RSF and all of Caligula's army are on their own.

Inside, the war is still raging as well, with the RSF and the 'Hoarder's' not ready to give up. The smell of death and destruction is all around the city. Caligula has still not even come out of his dwelling, secure against the onslaught.

The revolution wages on through the night, with the numbers still on the side of the rebels and those who need it rest, while their replacements pick it up. The next day the fighting is still continuing, but now there is an enormous shift within the RSF, realizing that they are killing off the same rodents they are supposed to defend, many of them deflect and join the resistance. This has a huge change on the already outnumbered RSF. They have no other choice but to retreat. This is just what Madison has been waiting for.

With the last blockade to the 'Rodent Leader' now shattered, the rodents charge in take Caligula. A chorus calling for the hang-rat's noose is heard in the swarm of rodents. One amongst them is more than happy to oblige, and sets up the gallows. As the mob is carrying him to the meet his fate, Madison sprints as fast as he can to cut them off.

"NO!- We can't do this. Not this way, not like this. We are the rodents of civility and you're proposing murder. He needs to be tried formally and fairly by the Senators. That's the laws here, if we abandon them now, at this such dark an hour, all is lost."

There is murmurs of dissention and grumbling by the

crowd, but then Washington steps forward.

"Madison is correct. We can't commit a murder, not if
we want all we have accomplished together to stay of the value
that we hold it. He must be tried, in a court of law."

So instead of the gallows, Caligula is thrown in jail, as
well as his cohorts and heads of the departments, awaiting trial.

T he next day **Madison and** some of the other

rodents, Nero included, go and sift through the city for
survivors. Included in the dead are Kerry, both the dogs,
Gorby, Caesar, Rockefeller, Shakespeare, Reid, Gibbs, many
of the RSF, the pigeons and drones number are dramatically
cut, only a few of the sparrows on both sides remain, none of
the hummingbirds survive, the mice and chipmunk squads
are no more, Plato, and Monroe, are also among the dead.

The dead are given their respective funerals and the rest
of the day is a day of silence for them. Madison commissions
the building of a memorial with the names of the dead be
made.

"You mean the 'Originals' dead right," comments a
member of the crowd.

"No, I mean every animal that lost it's life. It's time that
we do operate as a real society, and not embrace such divisive
tactics. We can disagree with each other, but we need to keep

85

an open mind to the other opinions and come to a compromise when needed. An agreement that benefits both sides, both need to give, in order to get. Let's start with this monument. It's what Jefferson would have wanted," Madison responds.

"He's right," Carnegie chimes in, "we all bleed here last night. It's the only way to bring peace to the Colony. I will put up my resources to help with it, and I encourage the other industrials to follow suit."

"Only if they want, and whatever amount they want," Madison comments, "we can't have a repeat of this 'Class Warfare' rhetoric. The 'Industrials' should not be demonized, but praised for their contributions to the Colony. They give their time, resources, and strength, to make our society succeed. Let's honor the dead, by learning to work together."

That's what they do all of the rodents working together to clean up the pathways and it's dwellings, commercial and residential. Much of the dwellings suffer from fire damage and have to be destroyed. The left over propaganda is taken down and burned outside of the city. All the remnants of Caligula's reign of terror have been destroyed.

T he next two weeks are spent searching through

the rubble at the library, for anything that could link Caligula or his associates to the wreckage. Before his death, Gorby made a formal statement about the disturbance he witnessed there two nights before, than something happens that changes everything for the better in the case.. The device that started the fire, was turned in. It turns out the night I question a packrat, Nicolas, found it and hoarded it. Word reached him of what happened there, and he brought it in to be examined by the tribunal.

After they determined it was in fact what started the fire, then they started asking around to see if any rodent had seen or heard anything from that night. A witness did come forward, but refused to testify. They found evidence at the scene that the assassin had left and interrogated him, he cracked and the whole conspiracy was revealed. Caligula, the judges, the Senators and Statesrats involved, and the RSF, that had survived would now face justice.

The trial only lasted two weeks, the jury was made up of 'Working Rodents', from neither the 'Hoarders' or the 'Originals'. The defense was adamant about the fact that, Caligula (calling him Gaius, during the trial of course) had done nothing wrong, and since he was elected by the rodents he was in his rights to keep his position. That they were, in fact, the ones who had performed illegal acts. It was a disgraceful and fruitless effort in the end.

Even in an unbiased courtroom, the atrocities by him could not be ignored and the prosecutors proved their claim of treason easily. The only rodent not even on trial was Soros, there was nothing that connected him to any wrongdoing. He was proven to do some sketchy things, but illegal, no.

Of those on trial most of them, the Senators, the judges, and the Statesrats, got 'Life Captivity' and would never see freedom again. As for Caligula, the assassin, and a couple of the Senators and Statesrats, got the 'Death Consequence,' to be enforced in two days. Madison of all rodents requested that it be reversed to the lesser penalty, but the judge and jury overruled him. In two days the tyranny of Caligula and his forces would be no more.

While awaiting his hanging, Caligula gets the most unexpected visitor; Madison comes in to see him. If he is surprised by this it doesn't show, his face is as hard as it had been during the trial. No longer does that sickly sweet, exaggerated smile grace his face. No longer is his arrogant and friendly manner exuding from him. No longer does he have the right thing to say and for once, he is saying nothing at all.

"Caligula, you should know that I still believe that you don't deserve to be put to death for what you've done. I know that Jefferson would not have agreed with me on that… I don't honestly know that that isn't the best thing for all of us, but I just can't feel good about killing another rodent, even if it's justified.

So maybe you can help me with this.. Do you have a civil side? Do you feel any remorse for what you've done?"

A smile crosses his face for the first time in weeks, and he laughs. "What should I feel sorry for? Trying to build this Colony into an empire.. Trying to make sure we all have a little piece of the pie? This should not be hard for you to understand, you are a smart rodent. All rodents are social animals and need to be lead. You all need to be told what to do and how to do it. I'm the only one who showed he was willing to do so," Caligula replies.

"What about you, doesn't that mean you should be lead as well. I think, I just got my answer and I understand Jefferson's stance on this. Tyranny is punished by death, it seems a fitting end."

"I would have done it to you, maybe that will change your mind. I would kill each and everyone of the Senators, Statesrats and 'Industrials,' that came between me and 'Rodentopia.' But first I would have gotten rid of each and every human being. I don't feel sorry for my actions, I didn't go far enough in this cause."

"Why?... Why do you hate the humans so much?"

"Why? WHY? Why would I not?... They ruin our society, they kill us without a second thought, they run the planet into oblivion. We would be extinct if they had their way, and you 'Originals,' want to reach a commerce with them. You and I do know that won't happen."

"I don't see that happening.. I will give you that, but that doesn't mean that Jefferson's plan for the Colony is wrong. You condemn the humans for how they treat us, that does not validate our doing the same to them. That would makes us just as wrong. In the universe they are just a blip, so that makes us a micro-blip. We have no right to cause the extinction of another species. That is a comment you made when the human genocide was first considered by other rodents. How do you live with this level of hypocrisy?"

"Don't lecture me, you filthy vermin," Caligula snarls back, "one who speaks for the 'Working Rodents' .. One who claims to be of the common rodents, you call me a hypocrite… Yet you try to represent both sides, you can't. It's not feasible."

"So you feel that you are of the common rodent? Spending their hard earned food stocks on projects that they disagree with. Living in luxury, while your fellow rodent is struggling, because of your laws. Or your attitude about the 'Domesties.' They are our friends and colleagues and instead you call them out, it doesn't make sense."

"Yes.. Because you don't know anything about living in a cage," Caligula replies.

"You do!.." Madison snaps back, not getting a reaction, he changes that to a question. "Do you?… Is that why you hate the humans so much? Were you a mistreated pet?.." Caligula's eyes narrow and a low growl comes from his mouth. "Were you a lab rat, maybe? In a zoo of some kind?"

"ENOUGH! I will not be your social experiment. I will not help you understand the secrets of civility. My past is my own, and I don't have to tell you anything."

"I know.. And I agree, but then why did ask that from others? Why did you make up your past? The rodents of the Colony do have the right to know who they elected and what he stood for." With that last comment, he walks away.

T he next day is the day of the executions and they

are showing just what type of rodents they really are. They are all crying and sniffling, all except for Caligula, he is so full of rage that he shows very little emotion in fact. Caligula gets to savor this as he is the last to hang and by himself.

After all this a special election for 'Rodent Leader' and this time all the 'Groups' get equal representatives. Madison and Nero find one that represents everything that Jefferson would have wanted in a 'Liberodent', the party that has taken the best of both the 'Originals' and the 'Hoarders.'

The put their full support behind the rodent of this 'Group' , a rodent named Hancock.

CHAPTER TEN:

REPAIRING THE

DAMAGE

The special election has a very short campaign, only

two months and it's one that has a lot of information out there.
The non media outlets are making sure that the rodent citizens
don't repeat the same mistake. If history is any indication of the
possibilities for improvement, that is more than likely the wisest
course. Letting another dictator in now would be detrimental to
undoing Caligula's damage.

With the changes to the system, the other 'Groups' are
actually able to compete. Compete they do, all of them have a

couple of representatives at first, than it gets dwindled down, to one of each.

The 'Hoarder' Kennedy Jr. is a young but fair rat, Washington represents the 'Originals', the 'Industrials' start their own party and are represented by Carnegie, Hancock for the 'Liberodents', and the Squirrels start their own party with Cassino, a fire tempered older veteran from the squirrel wars with views similar to the 'Originals,' for its representative.

This election takes on a life of it's own and is actually very civil, almost like the other opinions of the other 'Groups,' being thrown into the pot might be what was needed all along. Some of the 'Originals' and the 'Hoarders' argue that with the others in there take votes from their 'Group', but the evidence of this is slim and those in support of the others participation report it as being helpful to the elections as a whole.

The end result is the unheard of event of the first other 'Group' getting in, with the election of the Liberodent, Hancock.

The Senators and Statesrats have been arguing against Hancock from the beginning, because of his stances on the cozy relationship between the 'Alliance' bosses, corrupt 'Industrials,' and the Senators and Statesrats. They make up other reasons to condemn him of course. But he has been saying that he is going to 'clean up the filth in the rat's nest.' That is what he does too. All the corruption that has been allowed to fester when the Colony was under the 'Hoarders' and 'Originals,' is now being dissolved. Those involved in the moral decay are prosecuted for ethics violations. Soros has long since abandoned the Colony, this time banished for his part in Caligula's reign.

The regulations on the industries in the Colony are cut back, and in most cases just eliminated. The 'Rodent-ment' departments are evaluated and the ones that don't work are either fixed to make them more efficient or are disbanded and closed. The heads of them are investigated for impropriety and those found guilty are remanded into 'captivity.'

He replaces the entitlements system that had been running rampant with an incentive system that offers everyone in the Colony the same opportunities and has even better rewards than the previous system. Better yet it is a system that has a sustainable mechanism to it and won't have to worry about needing more funding.

So the healing has begun, it's slow at first as expected but within a couple of months, it has picked up speed and prosperity in the Colony has expanded to an unimaginable degree.

A **year has now passed since** Hancock's election and there has been a sorrowful event, Madison died after a month long battle with pneumonia. He was laid to rest next to his mentor, Jefferson. When his mate goes through his things, she finds a couple of letters, one addressed to her and the other with instructions to be given to Hancock should he die during his administration. She promptly sends it to the 'Rodent

Leader.' Hancock calls a press conference.

"Last week, we suffered a deep blow.. The last of our founders, Statesrat Madison passed on. In his effects, his mate found a letter addressed to the Colony. I shall now read it:

To the United Rodents of the Manhattan Colony,

It has always been my honor to call myself your representative, it has always been the greatest joy of my life. I have not always walked with the courage of my friend and mentor, Jefferson, when the Colony was in it's worst crisis he went into the den of death and found common ground with the cat Gorby. I entered there with doubt and fear, but I have always tried to do what I feel is best for the rodents here.

I have never put myself first. I think he would have been proud of me for that, at least I hope so. I tried to conduct myself in the manner that he would have. In the Colony, our greatest triumphant, I have learned much and one of the greatest lessons I can teach is this. It is so important to make sure that all your dealing are done in a way that is fair not only to others, but also to yourself. Do not let anyone decide for you your fate, make it yourself. If you don't have your own dream, help someone else with theirs.

Charity and community at the small scale are the most crucial driving points of prosperity, and letting someone else tell how to ruin your own affairs, someone who doesn't know the pressures and expenses, hasn't had those many sleepless nights, or made those hard choices, is in a word "Criminal."

In closing I will just say that there will be a time, when humans will meet their ends. It might not be for hundreds or thousands of years, but it will be the inevitable conclusion. At that time another species of the animal kingdom will have to step up to fill that void. That species will be us. At that point we will have to stand on our own two paws. We need to be prepared for this, that is why it is so important to make sure that we know who we are as individual rodents, so we know our place in the society we have, now and in the future.

I hope that long after I'm gone, prosperity will continue and this, our Manhattan Colony, will flourish for a very long time. With love in my heart and soul, forever your servant.

Madison Rat

Jefferson Rat"

96

THE END

AUTHOR'S

COMMENTS

There has been this attitude that has been allowed
to run amok, completely unfettered and even encouraged at
times, by those who are supposed to guard the public against
such dangerous inclinations. This attitude is one of entitlement
and that it's immaterial what the moral consequences of the
policies on the people are, as long as there are 'good intentions'
behind the decisions. Why is this wrong? The expression that
explains it best is: *The road to hell, is paved with good
intentions.*

This is not a warning of those who are trying to improve
the world, but a warning **for** those who are trying to improve the
world. The Occupy Wall Street crowd, the environmental
activists, the gay rights supporters, the pro-choice crowd, etc.,
this message is for you. Your actions for your cause not only,

have an impact on how many supporters you can enlist, but also how receptive the public is to you and your cause. Even those who are against you because of moral objection, will at least listen to you, if you express yourself in the right manner. There is a difference between; peaceful protest and civil disobedience, and anarchy and destruction of property. What you do matters just as much as what you stand for.

That is not the only part of the issue of what needs to be pointed out for consideration though. The other part is that this attitude of 'Moral Superiority' is one that is easily manipulated. If you follow this trend you make yourself a pawn of the politicians. Look at the causes that the politicians have made their own pet projects and the end results as far as public perception is concerned at least.

The 'Green Movement,' has been a Public Relations nightmare because of government involvement. Why? In part because the government wants to spend money so they can increase their power, which means they keep all the facets of the movement rather than implementing the beneficial ones and abandoning the harmful portions. With this lack of spending discipline comes contempt from the taxpayers who want to see their tax money spent responsibly. Here's a bit of advice for all you activists- Don't let your causes become a federal mandate. When the bill comes back for the venture and hit's the taxpayer, then the disenchantment will begin and they will want heads to roll. Yours' will be on the chopping block as well!

That is why I wrote this book. I'm not a Republican or

Democrat, but a Libertarian, and I want this country to be the best it can be. Neither of the two major parties will fix the problems of this country, because most of the problems come from the two party system. It's basically a game of tag, either with the establishment of the Republicans or the Democratic party being 'it.' Both the Obama and Bush administrations are evidence of this. If you examine their presidencies without 'party goggles' on, you will notice that both have similar policies and that many of Obama's are in fact the enlarged versions of Bush's stances.

Now we are almost at a time for another election, Mitt Romney is poised to be our next president. This is not going to be a monumental point in history, but monumental points in history are more times than not ones in which are times of suffering. That is why I'm not in favor of such an agenda, change for the sake of change. This doesn't make things better, it just makes them different. How is that better than what Hitler created, or Stalin, or Attila the Hun? How is this an improvement? Shouldn't that be what we should strive for, rather than simply change, but a practical change instead.

For the most part I wouldn't have expected a real change, because it's not something that is in the agenda of most of the politicians. Most are just satisfied with just maintaining the status quo and are less concerned with rectifying the damage done by the progressives of the past hundred plus years as much as securing their positions. That mindset is why things as they are right now will not change, we the people need to help the change along. We need to remember that the people have all the power and remind those who think they are in power of that fact.

First, they need to be reminded that they, more than anyone need to hold strictly to the United States Constitution especially if they want to come up with a fair solution to the problems of the day. This document is the most unbiased source for the laws of the land ever written and has just as much relevance today. Keep in mind the individuals who wrote the Constitution, the Declaration of Independence, and the Bill of Rights, also set the ground work for the greatest country on the face of the planet. Their foresight should not be undervalued, especially by who show such signs of delusions of grandeur or narcissism. Also don't fall for this trap of undervaluing the country itself, there is nothing wrong with being proud of this country. That it exists at all is basically an impossibility, the odds were not in our country's favor remember.

Second, we have to remember just because the one who represents us gets into office it doesn't mean that we can let our guard down. It's the responsibility of the people to make sure that they do what is in the best interest of the people not for their own interest. The policies they set have to keep the country secure, encourage job growth, and withhold the ethical standards and rights in the written documents of the founders.

Third, we can not encourage divisive politics. Personally I don't want the two major parties to be in agreement. The end result of this is almost always worse than them being in contention. The reason for this is simple, when they disagree there is a debate and when that happens than an exchange of ideas occurs and a practical solution can be reached because all sides of the issue have been considered. That is not the same thing as being divisive though. Divisive is taking a stance that is controversial, just to malign the other side, not to pick on the Democratic Party, but that seems to be the stance your representatives have chosen. For the most part democrats don't seem to want to debate. They want to make a clear line in the sand, and exclude those who disagree from the discussion. It's not a surprise really though, the party was formed to be the antagonist for the republican party. Andrew Jackson didn't feel the republicans were doing what was in the best interests of the people, (it was the large government supporters at that time) and the Whigs which was the other party at the time, wasn't much better, so he created the democratic party. Known as the party of the people at the time it was but that has long since changed. Of course since the progressive party's founding under Theodore Roosevelt, neither has been entirely true to the people they are supposed to serve. Both have become parties of the policy and left the people out in the cold. Both care more about tearing down the opposing party, than rebuilding this country to it's former glory. Both are right and both are wrong, on the issues.

REFERENCES

During **World War II, British** citizen George Orwell, wrote his classic satire *Animal Farm*. His book has been in print numerous times including a couple of illustrated versions.

My first exposure to this work was when in 1999 TNT aired a Hallmark production of the classic. The 1999 is a live action production, including voices of Patrick Stewart, Kelsey Grammar, and Julia Louis Dreyfus, among the talents. There is also an animated version as well, that plays out as basically a propaganda style film.

The concept of the story revolves around an English farm that gets taken over by the animals, being lead by the greedy pigs on it. It makes comparisons that of what was going on in Soviet controlled Russian, under Stalin. Many of the animals are symbolic of the specific people involved, while others are symbols of the different social classes.

Fast forward to the present, and we have a time of turmoil that has some similarities to those dark days of history, when dictators ruled. *Animal* Farm was the initial inspiration for this book. One of thing I should mention is that this is one of the view times I liked the movie (the 1999 version) more than the book.

Not to say that George Orwell didn't create an insightful and thought provoking classic, but it was in my opinion incomplete in explaining what was wrong with Russian style socialism but not giving a contrast between socialism and capitalism.

It wasn't until later that I found out why, George Orwell was a socialist himself, and like many other socialist countries he felt that the basic theory of socialism does work. I also read a book about a Jewish German woman who survived Nazi Occupied Germany, who was under this impression as well. All these people think that their versions of these political systems will work. Well I respectfully disagree. Then I found a series of You-Tube videos, where a defected Soviet Russian talks to a group of Americans about socialism and communism. Making sure to impress upon them the unadulterated truth about how insidious, such schools of thought really are. This served only to validate my opinion.

The problem with both philosophies, is they work under the assumption that government can do what the people can't.

The limits of what the people can do, doesn't exist. It you can dream someone, somewhere can make it a reality. I have complete and total faith that the free market system can work if it is left to itself, rather than interventionist policies by it's leaders. Fact is, the large government system has never worked and doesn't work, history shows this. This idea that if we only did tried it we could make it work is something that dictators are counting on. How arrogant of modern people to think that other empire's citizens before them have not thought of that.

The contempt of the capitalist system is itself based on the lie that we have been living in a unhindered, free market system. Truth is the last time we had a real free market system was under President Grover Cleveland.

Those who do subscribe to this idea are under the impression that it can be accomplished without a dictator, is also not true. Many will resist it the obliteration of capitalism, so that is impossible.

Now when you read this book, you will see that some of the characters are based on real people, but some might not be recognized. Like in *Animal Farm*, I have characters that are based on real people and others on certain class roles in society, or philosophies and ideas.

The role of Jefferson for example, he's a symbol of industry and moral clarity. Unwavering from what is clearly right and wrong, he doesn't kowtow to the special interests or even to a 'group,' and will tell his 'group,' the 'Originals' off if needed. My main model for him is a mixture of the Roman lawyer Cicero and Ron Paul. He also is the closest representative of myself in the book. When I first conceptualizing the story, Jefferson didn't get killed. After I came up with a specific function for him however, he had to, to be true to the reality of the situation. I should note though, it

107

was one of the hardest part of the book for me to write.

Madison is also based on a concept more than anything, he is a symbol, of renewed faith in mankind, country, and a cause. He starts off a little unsure of himself and the Colony at times, but loyal and true to the cause. As the freedom and rights of his fellow rodents are getting dismantled by the over zealous Gaius, his fire for independence makes him leap into action.

Another symbolic creature is the Hawk. It represents government interventionist policies. The suffocating federal regulations on business, the nationalized healthcare systems, for examples.

Soros is the symbol of crony capitalism and corruption, in the relationship between business and government. He is the puppet master, who hides away from the world, and controls things from his perch.

Gorby is the symbol of political compromise. The same kind of relationship that the real Gorbachev and Reagan had. Both sides have to give, or else it's not an authentic compromise. A reality in politics that is usually ignored.

There are real people represented in the book as well though. Adams, is George W. Bush. When I started writing this I was originally going to call him Hancock. I later changed my mind because Bush was considered a disappointment by people, and as a president I feel that John Adams was as a president as well.

Gaius, represents Barack Obama. The king of Hype, the used car salesman of the world of politics. In the part where I reveal that he has another name, some reading this might be thinking this a commentary about the birth certificate that's not it. That claim might have some factual basis in it, but it's not really that incident it's based on, no. What I'm commenting on has to do with the Barry Soetoro issue, for those who don't know, Barack Obama's birth certificate is said to be under this name. He didn't change it to his deadbeat father's name until later and was known Barry Soetoro before then. He also didn't have anything other than the testimony of professors and other supposed classmates that he attended as a student, or was employed, at the schools he said he was. He has no paper trail, just hearsay. That should be very troubling for people. Also disconcerting is the fact that to keep this up he has had to perpetrate identity theft.

Bain is Mitt Romney. Sanatorium is Rick Santorum. Newt is Newt Gingrich. Pelousy is Pelosi. Holder is Eric Holder. Hancock, is another that's not based on an individual, but on an idea. The introduction of the third parties, as serious contenders into the political arena.

Nero is a symbol really as well, in the end. He is the symbol of those in his party disenfranchised by their despotic authority figures. The leaders who have drawn a line in the sand, not expecting their most resolute supporters to abandon them.

The other major influence to this book is *The Prince,* with it's condemnation of aristocracy and the importance of being true to those you serve. That is also a political virtue that many have tossed aside by the elite, that it's the people that have the power, not them. The influence of this is seen throughout the story, but is blatantly obvious in the last few chapters.

Not on the list that some might think influenced this piece of literature, is the *Maus* graphic novel series and *The Secret of Nihm*. Other than the anthropomorphized rodents, there's really no connection to my story. I am familiar to both stories though.

When I wrote this story I had to look up Barack Obama and I found out he did actually do more than just Obamacare, none of it was worth anything though. Like a typical bureaucrat, he had to make it look like he was doing anything, whether it was actually beneficial or not. That is what he had planned for his first term, his second is when he will implement his plans to change the country to the socialized Europe version of America. I implore those who might read this, who think that socialism is a benevolent, humane social structure to talk to someone who knows first hand. I do believe that if Obama wins again, that is the path for our country. That's the bad news, the good news as I see it, is that we can get through it. The other countries have, and ours is so much stronger. I do have faith in that. What I described in the last couple of chapters is something that I hope we don't have to go through though. It's basically needless suffering.

In the end I do believe that the only way that we will create a real positive change to prosperity is to abandon the two party system. Letting in the other parties brings in new perspectives on the issues and as a side effect more clarity.

Many have given up on this country, this story was told to help restore faith in it. To quote a couple of my favorite rodents, *'I hope that long after I'm gone, prosperity will continue and this, our Manhattan Colony, will flourish for a very long time. With love in my heart and soul, forever your servant.'*

Madison Rat

Jefferson Rat

R. C. Seely, the Author

R. C. SEELY
PRESENTS ...

AMERICANUSLIBERTAE

On twitter and check out my blog on wordpress.com

www.ingramcontent.com/pod-product-compliance
Lightning Source LLC
Chambersburg PA
CBHW072316290526
45794CB00002B/679